THE DIVIDEND INVESTING BLUEPRINT

BY

DALE WALTON

Contents

Introduction

A lot of the time, quite a number of people seem to get themselves worked up on how to boost their finances. Many people want to break free from "not having enough money" but they just simply don't have the knowledge on how to go about it. According to a study, the issue of not being financially buoyant has led quite a number of people to depression.

Has this ever been a problem you've had before? Well if it is, don't worry. Many people have been in your shoes, just sit back, relax, and enjoy the financial enlightenment this book will provide you with.

In this book, I'll explain all you need to know about having a money mindset, how to say goodbye to lack of money, and also the exact steps and strategies to get started investing in dividends.

I've written this book to help you understand how to be a good investor, how to avoid the pitfalls people fall into, and how to build that passive income we all dream of.

My father never knew the secrets behind investing until he had just ten years to retire. He kept saying he wished he had known earlier. My father has lived with this regret all his life despite making good use of this secret regardless of the time he discovered it. He practically lives large as a retiree right now (6 years after retirement) without having to sweat or work anymore.

You will understand the beauty of investing in dividends as well as the essential things you need to know about creating multiple streams of income. Our major focus in this book is investing in dividends. So many times, a lot of people work so hard, craving a lot of money yet earning very little. It took me several years to finally discover that what sets the rich apart from the poor actually lives in their mind and mentality.

I once told a man to ensure his next generation starts saving as early as 10 and he just didn't understand where I was coming from until I had shared some of these "financial truths" with him.

If your aim in life is to work really hard and continue to work until you are above eighty and old and wrinkled, leaving your family with nothing but your payslips to live with when you are gone, please do not read this book. However, if your desire is to leave your family a legacy when you are gone and ticking off your bucket list while you are retired, this book is for you.

There's a feeling of fulfillment that comes with living off all you worked hard for, while you are retired and no longer working. The feeling that comes with having your investments work for you is simply unbeatable.

While you may not end up having your name on Forbes list as the richest man on the planet, having the key to success as well as being a successful investor would definitely earn you much more than "money". How about the respect that comes with being an "investment guru?" For certain reasons, if you crave real success, you have to read this book.

The millennial generation doesn't seem to be interested in investing and as much as we think the act of investing is fading away, thousands of people are still earning loads of money from investing. It's never too late to step up your game and become the next most successful investor.

You will find in this book all the latest information you need to know about dividend investing as well as relevant information discovered from personal experiences of successful investors which would definitely help you make only the best decisions. Some people have failed several times while trying to invest; the personal experiences of these people have been compiled to let you know the kind of things you shouldn't do as an investor.

One of the numerous things you have to look forward to learning is the power of compounding; how to make a real profit from compounding, how companies pay dividends, how to understand a perfect pay-out ratio, how long you should hold stocks as well as the general misconceptions about dividends.

You will also learn the crucial terminologies and language of investing and the stock market, and how investing goes beyond something that can be understood without in-depth understanding.

This book is designed and written to prepare you towards every obstacle you might come across in the investing world. Failure to read this beginner-friendly book would cost you more damage than you could imagine as you might never learn the right way to invest and also never come across these "secrets to building your finances".

I have personally applied the tips in this book, and I must say that although I have made certain mistakes in life as an investor and lost a lot of money on poor investments through lack of education, my financial security and status have never been better.

Chapter 1

BECOMING FINANCIALLY AWARE

In this chapter, you will learn how to become financially aware. Quite a number of people do not feel the need to invest, because they have little to no knowledge of how to increase their finances and up their financial game. What do I mean by this? Financial awareness will liberate you from poverty.

If you think you are wealthy but have no knowledge about the secret to financial freedom, your wealth would definitely not last a lifetime. Do not be surprised, this is simply because people who have genuine wealth and those who are successful with money do not enjoy spending money; they enjoy making it. If you do not understand this and happen to be a spendthrift or you always find yourself exceeding your budget and going beyond your financial limits, you need to read on. Now, it doesn't matter how many financial errors you have made or how many regrets you have, this chapter will help you rectify every error and prepare you to become really better at investing.

At the end of this chapter, you would have known the difference between having an active income and the need to build a passive income through investing in reasonable assets.

The truth about investing is that those who got the idea of investing earlier have one regret in life. What regret do you think they have? Well, the only regret they have is "not starting earlier". What this tells you is, it's never too early to start investing, you are not too young to understand what the world of investment looks like and how to go about it the perfect way. A lot of people need answers to this golden question:

Why should we Invest? There are lots of reasons you ought to invest. However, you might be wondering if *investing* and *saving* mean the same thing. Well, let's try to clarify that. Saving and investing are two entirely different things, although a lot of people try to substitute them with each other and often mistake the two for the same thing. Investing can be defined according to Wikipedia as, the act of allocating money in the expectation of some benefit in the future. In other words, it can be defined as an act of growing your money or making your money appreciate while setting it aside for future purposes.

Now, what is **SAVING?** A lot of economists believe that saving is simply the act of spending less in the present, in order to spend abundantly in the future. Saving can further be defined as the act of putting aside an amount of money which you do not have plans for at the moment, for emergencies, or for a future purpose.

The difference between saving and investing is that the money you set aside to save has to be an amount of money you want to be able to access quickly with little or no risk, and with a very little amount of taxes.

You might keep a particular amount of money in your piggy bank, under your mattress, or somewhere in your apartment. Such money can also be kept in a financial institution for a certain period of time, which is mostly a short time. This is because you do not have plans to spend the money at the moment but would like to reach such money easily when an emergency calls for it, or when the need arises.

On the other hand, investing basically means the act of acquiring assets such as stocks, mutual funds, or real estate, with the prospect of making money from such investments in the nearest future. Most investments are made for the sole purpose of achieving long-term goals. Now that you know the difference between investing and saving, you should understand the benefits of investing.

Why do you need to invest and grow your money?

We all need money for our day-to-day activities. Money is an essential part of human life and just like human life itself, you need to grow your money. The very moment a person stops growing is the moment such a person stops existing. If you fail to grow your finances, the death of your financial life is certain.

A lot of millionaires and billionaires wake up every day to think of how to multiply their money, how to expand their finances, and invest in more business opportunities. I will tell you the story of a young man who inherited a whooping sum of money. This young man was richer than the head of state at that time and was envied by all. The only mistake he made was relying on this cash he had at hand; he got himself more liabilities than assets. He had a fleet of modern cars which required regular maintenance. He also slept in five-star hotels, and within two years, guess what happened? The money was gone in no time at all.

The point here is, it doesn't matter how much or how little you have, it's certain you can improve your financial status if only, you would master the art of investing. The good news is that successful investors didn't wake up one morning to become successful; they practiced the art of investing and became experts. You can become an excellent investor as well.

One mistake a lot of people make with money is believing in the current value of money, without considering how the rate of inflation can rise beyond the current value of your money. Also, It's high time we stopped depending on the government. One reason you need to start investing now is that the government might just go bankrupt if nobody decides to grow their own money.

Other reasons you need to invest and grow your money are as follows:

❖ **To earn an amazing return:** A lot of people invest their money in order to earn an amazing return. This basically means that one of the reasons for investing money is to gain something higher than your initial capital. You have to invest your money in a place where you can get a high rate in return. When there is an increase in your return, you will most definitely earn more money as well. Unlike saving, investing your money provides an opportunity to earn higher rates of return as well as interest. Therefore, if you would like to get a higher return on your money, it is advisable to invest such money instead of saving it.

❖ **To create a legacy:** It is the onus of a responsible parent to create a legacy for his/her children and family. One reason you need to invest your money in assets is to create a legacy when you leave. The last thing you want is to leave your family to suffer when something happens in the future. One amazing way to leave a legacy behind you is to start investing for the future when you are still young, agile, and able. A lot of people who have done this in the past have made their family happy while others who didn't feel the need to save when they were younger often grow up into old people who regret not making the decision of investing while they were younger. There are different options out there such as estates, stocks, shares, and mutual funds, which would definitely appreciate in the future and earn more money.

❖ Retirement: **Why should you save for retirement?** Retirement is an inevitable part of human life. It is the period you have to step down from work or give up on work. Whether we like it or not, the truth is that the human body isn't designed to work forever; this is as a result of declining skills, health, and other factors that come with old age. This period is a crucial part of your life and a huge reason you should take the issue of investing seriously. One reason why you should invest for retirement is to sit back and make your money "work" for you. Before retirement, you'd have spent so many years working around the clock in order to make money; post-retirement should, therefore, be a time when all the money accumulated over the years should do the "work" for you. It is indeed a time you should sit back and enjoy your hard-earned money. While it is believed that retirement is meant for old and inactive people, a lot of people have broken this myth by retiring early after investing enough money for their retirement. It is indeed an achievement to retire at 40 or below such age. A certain man named Jeremy Jackson retired at the age of 38 after saving up fifty percent of his income for ten years. Another man named Todd Tresidder also retired at the age of 35 after investing for 12 years. It's not impossible for you to retire early, as long as you imbibe the culture of investing. The story of these early successful retirees tells you that you need to start investing for the sake of retirement if you do not want to run out of money in the future. Everyone has certain expectations in life, one of such expectations is having a bucket list. Some people also happen to have exotic dreams in life. Sometimes you want to explore what the world looks like, visit iconic places, purchase certain things in life and so on. Almost everyone would like the thought of having a vacation in Paris, while cruising in a yacht with champagne in your hand and a big smile on your face; living your best life, off your investments without working for a dime anymore. The best time to do these things you have always wanted to do and also tick off your bucket list is after retirement. In order to have this life you have always wanted, you need to start investing when you are young, to have something to fall back on, retire early, and also live a fancy life after retirement. One other reason you should invest for the purpose of retirement is to ensure that you do not become a burden on your loved ones after retirement. It is not a good idea to live your post-retirement life, depending on your family for survival. While this would earn you less respect, it might also not provide you the kind of life you have always wanted as the rest of your life would be spent depending on people for survival. You can also save yourself from going to an early grave, if you choose to invest for the purpose of retirement as failure to do this might just make you continue working and stressing yourself when you are grey and old. This is the period you should be resting and not working as any work you do at this stage of your life may cause your health to deteriorate and confine you to the sick bed for the rest of your life. A lot of health problems also come with old age; it is the reason you should invest in assets in case of emergencies in the future. You might also need to provide for your family after retirement. Since no pension can replace your salary, the best way to provide your family with a good life after retirement is to invest and make a living, off your investments. Finally, retirement should be the best time of your life; you would not be working for a very long time. Not having enough money can lead you to depression and frustration. The only way to save yourself from such is to invest for the future while you are still working.

❖ **Establish a business:** For some people, the purpose of investing is to establish a business, venture into new businesses, or develop an existing business. You can choose to invest in order to support a growing business or establish your own business. It is never wrong to have more than one source of income. Having multiple sources of income, on the other hand, will help you become financially stable. Investing in small businesses also affords you the opportunity to buy an ownership stake. While investing in other people's businesses can earn your financial freedom, it also helps you impact other people's lives as well.

❖ **Urgent funds:** One important reason you should invest is for the purpose of urgent or emergency funding. You never know what's going to happen the next minute. A lot of people have experienced unexpected/unforeseen events and circumstances such as a sudden layoff or setback from work. While it is good to be optimistic, you also need to prepare for the worst, just in case something unexpected happens to you or someone close to you. When such a situation arises, the best way to handle it is to have an emergency fund, which is one reason a lot of people invest. People invest for emergency purpose in order to save themselves from job loss, medical or dental emergency, unexpected home repairs, car maintenance, and unplanned vacation expenses. Although a lot of people do not feel any need to invest their emergency fund, one benefit you can earn is to hypothetically increase your net worth. Investing for emergency purpose will definitely save you from unnecessary stress as you can always have something to depend on when life brings something unexpected your way.

- ❖ **Time value of money**: When people invest, sometimes the only reason is "time value of money". What do I mean by this? The concept of time value in finance simply means that $1ooo at hand is worth more than the equivalent amount in the nearest future. This is simply because investing $1000 will definitely earn you much more in the future. The sooner you invest your money, the sooner it works for you because a thousand dollar now might lose the value it has, when acquired in the next few years. The main idea behind the concept of the time value of money simply means you need to invest now rather than later so as to grow your money over time and to also enjoy a long term compound interest.

Now that you already know the value of investing and the importance of investing, the next question is how much you should invest? "I want to invest but I'm confused about how to start and how much I need to begin with". If this is you, you have no cause to be worried. Although, there is no fixed amount to be invested as you need to do something convenient for you and not go beyond your limits. You should only invest an amount of money that won't stop you from sleeping at night. Only what you can afford to lose should be invested as you do not want to end up in the hospital when something unexpected happens. One great way to start investing is to start with the same amount you would usually save up monthly. If you are used to saving 20% of your income monthly, you might just decide to invest exactly the same amount monthly. However, I personally think that making a decision to invest has a lot to do with how much responsibilities you have, the amount of money you would invest if you were single would be totally different from the amount you would invest if you were married. The kind of goals you also want to reach in life and the time you plan to achieve such goals should also determine how much you would invest. For instance, if you plan to retire early (at a certain age), you need to invest more (a certain percent of your income) and spend less in order to reach your goal faster. Think of the kind of goals you have. Your goal might be to pay for your offspring's college education. If this is your goal, you need to know how much time you have before your child goes to college and invest towards this time by approximating a rational rate of return for your investment assortment. You can work towards this goal by investing just enough money every month. Calculating how much you need to save becomes really easy when your goals are defined and specific. There are also various calculators you can find online if you need to figure out exactly how much money you should set aside to reach your goal. If you also have the money you aren't using at the moment or any idle money you do not see yourself spending in the next few years, such money should be invested, as it would increase over time. The general idea about investing is to check your financial life. Once you are able to meet your goals and you have settled "every bill", the next thing is to invest everything you have to spare. Investing also depends on how much tax an individual pays; people who earn a lower income are expected to substitute an increased percent of their salary than folks who earn a higher income. This is because they are required to pay less tax and it isn't pragmatic to cut down if you are already on the breadline.

Diversifying of income

After understanding the importance of investing and what percentage of your income you need to invest, one other important concept you should understand is the importance of diversifying your income. Income diversification has to do with coming up with various revenue streams that are independent of each other. Diversification is a procedure that condenses risk by apportioning investments among numerous financial instruments, industries, and other classifications. It targets to capitalize on returns by investing in several areas that would each react contrarily to the same event. Several investment practitioners believe that although it does not guarantee against loss, diversification is the utmost essential component of attaining long-term monetary goals while abating risk. Our aim here is to explore the truth behind this and why you need to achieve diversification in your portfolio. Investors are often confronted with two focal kinds of risk when investing. The primary is undiversifiable, which is also the same as systematic or market risk. Every company is associated and connected with this kind of risk. This type of risk is often caused by an increase in inflation rates, exchange rate, political insecurity, war, and changes in interest rates. This type of risk is not actually particular to a specified company or industry, and such risks can never be eradicated or jettisoned through diversification. However, it is one kind of risk investors have to deal with.

The entire stock market is generally affected by systematic risk, not just a particular investment vehicle or industry is affected.

The subsequent kind of risk is diversifiable. This risk is also the same as unsystematic risk and is explicit to a company, industry, market, economy, or country. It can be reduced through diversification. The most rampant sources of unsystematic risk are business risk and monetary risk. Consequently, the aim of diversifying is to invest in several assets in order to avoid getting everything affected the same way by market happenings. Diversification also has a lot to do with going beyond your own geographical locations to source for several investment opportunities. Subsequently, the stocks and bonds in Europe may not be affected by volatility in the United States. This means investing in that part of the world may curtail and reduce the risks of investing in your own geographical location.

The concept of income diversification isn't a luxury or privilege; it is a necessity for everyone who has an intelligent attitude towards his/her finances. What is the concept of diversifying income? The concept of diversifying income simply means you need to have more than one source of income. In other words, it is basically the act of learning not to put all your eggs in a basket. Although, we sometimes get really comfortable with our income in life to the extent that we do not feel the need to diversify or have more than one income stream, this attitude of being really secure about your sense of income isn't the best. This is not about being pessimistic or expecting the worst to happen, it is, on the other hand, being financially alert and prepared for the worst. What am I trying to say here? I'm saying, no matter how fulfilling your job is, or how big your salary is, you need to have a side hustle or a side business just in case something unexpected happens. There are several ways you could work toward creating multiple streams of income. You might decide to set an hour or more than an hour each day in order to push for new sales, brainstorm about the kind of business you want to venture in asides from what you are doing presently. Look around you to see if there's any kind of service lacking in your environment or office and work towards providing such services. Don't be scared of attempting a new business; it's never a bad idea to try or risk something new. You can also source for jobs online, just to add to what you are already doing and also diversify your income. There are different digital data you can take advantage of, in order to discover new areas of revenue expansion.

There are several benefits that come with the diversification of income:

❖ **Maintenance of rising cost:** The rate at which the market cost of almost everything goes up these days is quite alarming, ranging from the price tag on your groceries to your tuition fee. Everything keeps easing beyond one's income by the day. The only way to cope with this increase in price is to have multiple sources of income. Diversifying Your income will not only help you maintain this rising cost, it would also ensure that the cost of living doesn't rise faster than your income.

❖ **Ability to afford huge purchases:** Think about how many times you have had to purchase a car or other expensive things on "loan". One benefit of diversifying your income is the ability to settle these bills and make these payments without adding them to your monthly bills. You can always pay cash for large purchases using your other sources of income.

Sometimes, you might be tempted to take out of your retirement fund or emergency fund in order to settle these bills if you depend solely on one source of income. You would save yourself from running into debt by expanding your sources of income.

❖ **Getting rid of job insecurity:** While this might be an obvious benefit, you need to understand that diversifying your income will definitely help you get rid of job insecurity. No matter how promising your job is, you can never tell what's going to happen tomorrow. When something unexpected happens like getting laid off from work, losing a potential client, or suffering any kind of unexpected risk, having something to fall back on would go a long way in helping your present condition. Although, these other income streams might not actually replace your "lost job", they would still help you maintain a normal life when combined with other opportunities/incentives that come with unemployment. The main idea is just to ensure you are doing "more" just in case something unexpected happens.

❖ **Elevating of lifestyle:** One great benefit of diversifying income is the opportunity it gives you to elevate your lifestyle. When you already have multiple streams of income, you might just decide to stop cutting down on your expenses in order to enjoy the benefits you have deprived yourself of. This doesn't mean you have to overspend all because you want to elevate your lifestyle. It doesn't mean you have to follow trends either; this only means you might choose to build a better lifestyle for yourself.

How to develop an investor's mindset?

To become a successful investor, you do not just wake up one morning with a decision to plunge into the stock market without having any knowledge on how to manage risks and how to develop a good attitude towards investing. It takes a very knowledgeable person in this area to take the decision of investing. One thing you have to understand is how crucial the human mind is when it comes to decision making. You are whatever you feed your mind. This is because what distinguishes you as a human being is your mind. Just like your fingerprints, your mind sets you apart from everyone else; this is exactly why two people will never think the same way at the same time or feel the same thing at the same time. To become an investor, especially a successful one, you need to develop the right mindset. It goes beyond psychology; it is simply the nature of humans to fail when they have designed their mind to fail or succeed when they have designed their mind to succeed. Sometimes, we can't help but wonder what goes wrong in our society; it's quite surprising to think that the rich keep getting richer while the poor keep getting poorer. This is only a result of their mentality. Your mindset goes a long way in making or marring you as an individual. How on earth do you expect to manage money efficiently if you can't manage your mind? That being said, here are the five key steps in developing an investor's mindset.

❖ **Get enlightened:** The very first thing you need to do while building an investor's mindset is to get yourself educated. It's quite easy to get swindled in this present world if you decide to invest without doing your research properly. The human mind can be developed through reading. You need to read extensively, take advantage of a lot of information available about investing online and understand exactly what investing entails. If you happen to be someone who doubts other people success stories, it would be a little bit difficult to change your mind, but this change of mind can occur when you get an education about investing and get yourself enlightened.

❖ **Reach out to investors around you:** One other way to develop an investor's mindset is to reach out to people who are successful investors around you. These people would help motivate you as well as provide you with the right information to get you started as an investor.

You might also select mentors and follow up with their stories while reaching out to them for motivation as well.

❖ **Be passionate about success:** There are certain people in life who just do not believe in having so much. As long as these people are able to afford their daily meals and put food on their table, they are fine. If you are one of these people, this kind of mindset will only drain every hope of becoming successful from you. In order to be an investor, you need to love money, love the idea of making money, and becoming successful. Of course, you should never get carried away with craving excess money. However, you need to genuinely love the idea of being successful. You need to enjoy the thought of having your money work for you to increase your net worth. This step is really crucial to developing an investor's mindset.

❖ **Watch your circle:** It is not a myth that the kind of people you spend quality time with have a great influence over you. If the people you spend time with happen to be skeptical about investing, there's a tendency that you may never become successful as an investor. This is because their mindset towards being successful will definitely rub off on you in one way or the other. In order to have the right attitude and attitude as an investor, you need to watch the kind of people you socialize with.

❖ **Accept losses:** The last but not the least step to developing an investor's approach is your ability to cope with losses and come to terms with losing as a necessary part of investing. You need to build your mind to accept the fact that investing comes with lots of risks, and coming to terms with this fact will also help you understand that you can minimize risks by investing the right way.

Sometimes we can't help but wonder why people go wrong and never make money. A lot of Americans basically live from pay-check to pay-check and you just never know why. Apart from not having an investor's mindset, there are also other reasons a lot of people will never make money. If they do not break free from these particular attitudes, they might never make it. Although money isn't actually everything and money will never replace happiness in the lives of human beings, we cannot underestimate the importance of money in our day to day lives. Money is a vehicle through which your goals can be achieved and our aim in this book is not to teach you how to make money; the purpose here is to teach you how to remain wealthy and maintain your wealth. Some of the reasons a lot of people never make money are as follows:

❖ **Economic illiteracy:** We have so many graduates out there who graduated with good grades but still find it difficult to make money. This is because academic literacy isn't the same as economic literacy. You could be learned yet remain an economic illiterate. This course isn't taught in schools/ colleges. Your professor would never teach you the pragmatic way to

33

become wealthy. It goes beyond having brilliant entrepreneurial skills. A young man recently paid a huge amount of money just to have lunch with Warren Buffet. A lot of people who do not know how intelligent the billionaire investor is would definitely insult this young man, but little do they know that this man indirectly paid for "knowledge". This is something a lot of us need to know. We need to learn how to boost our finances by understanding how your economy works.

❖ **Comparing your luck:** Until you stop getting comfortable with being broke, you might never enjoy the luxury of success. What do I mean by this? A lot of people find it really easy to say "I'm better than a lot of people". If you keep focusing on you being better than other people, without actually feeling there's a need to notice people who are way better than you, it becomes really difficult to make money. This is one reason why a lot of people never make money.

Until this mentality of comparing yourselves with others is abolished, the rich will only keep getting richer and the poor keep getting poorer.

❖ **Not owning up to your responsibilities:** Being dependent on other people for survival make it a little nerve-wracking to make your own money. I personally discovered that being independent actually motivates you to make your own money. As long as there's someone there who constantly gives you money, feed you, and provide you with shelter, you will not feel the need to make your own money. Living with your parents doesn't help you save money; it restricts you from opportunities. Until everyone begins to own up to certain responsibilities, people will always get it wrong when it comes to achieving real success.

❖ **Not getting out of your comfort zone:** I have discovered that I actually work best under pressure. The truth is we all want good things on a platter of gold. However, you need to know that it isn't a cliché to say that good things never come easily. If people would learn how to move out of their comfort zone, it becomes really easy to stay successful.

N.B: The purpose of this chapter is not to put you under any undue pressure to make money or overwork yourself to become successful. The purpose is to let you understand that you can actually achieve real success if you are determined to. The aim is to let you know that millions of people have made it; they achieved success after rising from nothing. You can do it too, if you understood the value of hard work and made good use of it, it would be really easy to make money.

Chapter 2

DIVIDEND STOCKS 101

What are dividends? A dividend is basically a kind of reimbursement made by a firm or organization to its shareholders, usually as dissemination or distribution of profits. A dividend is gotten from the Latin word divindendum (which means to be divided). After an organization earns a taking or profit, the corporation invests the money back into the business (this is known as retained earnings). Afterward, the corporation pays out a proportion of its surplus as a dividend to shareholders.

This payment to the shareholders may be in form of cash which is always deposited into the shareholder's bank account or if the corporation has a dividend reinvestment plan, the amount can be paid by the issue of further shares or share repurchase. This payment is circulated out of a firm's distributable profit. The percent amount to be shared to shareholders is a decision to be made by the board of directors; the board of directors comes together to hold a meeting in order to decide how much the cooperation pays out as "dividends" to shareholders. This decision is then approved by the shareholders.

Sometimes, the dividend is quoted in terms of the dollar quantity each share receives or sometimes, it is measured in terms of a percentage of the existing market price. Dividends can also be defined as a compulsory distribution of income and capital earnings a company realizes, which is paid to mutual fund investors. Different companies decide to pay dividends either yearly, quarterly, monthly, or other times convenient to the company.

One thing that makes dividends attractive to a lot of people is the fact that it is the only income of shareholders and the fact that you get to share out of the profit of a company without being directly involved in the business or selling.

Types of dividends

We have several types of dividends:

❖ Cash dividends: This is the most common form of dividends paid by most firms. This type of dividend is paid to the account of the shareholders via electronic funds transfer or a printed paper check. This dividend paid does not belong into the category of an expense; it is otherwise known as a deduction of retained earnings. It is the payment of cash directly to the shareholders. This dividend is paid on the declaration date by the company to the investors who still hold the company's stock on the indicated date. This date on which the dividends are allocated by the board of directors is known as the dividend date of record, while the day the payment of dividends is allotted to shareholders is known as the date of payment.

How does a cash dividend work? Let's assume you own 100 shares of Tianna's company. At the end of the quarter, Tianna's company calculates its financial performance for the quarter. This information is reviewed afterward by the board of directors, along with Tianna's company's profit margin. The board then declares a $0.10 dividend per share for the quarter. This simply means that you are actually eligible to $0.10 × 100 shares= $10.

❖ Stock dividends: This type of dividends is paid out in the form of a supplementary stock of the issuing corporation or a supplementary corporation. A company may decide to share this type of dividend to its shareholders when the company's liquid cash isn't really available. This is also known as scrip dividend and it is sometimes used in place of the cash dividend. A company may decide to give out this type of dividend because it wants to retain its cash for other purposes. The advantage this dividend has is that these stocks are not taxed until they are sold by an investor. How does this dividend work? Note that stock dividends are mostly allotted on the basis of percentage of prevailing holdings of stocks. For instance, let's assume that Tiana's company has made an announcement to allot this dividend of 30 percent. This infers that every individual who is a shareholder of the company will see their stock holding increase by 30 percent. So if you initially had 100 shares of Tianna's company, your share count after receiving your dividends will now be 130 in number.

❖ Property dividend: This particular type of dividend is different from cash and stock dividend. It is a type of dividend where the shareholders are rewarded with assets owned by the company. Such properties include portfolios, equipment or real estate. This kind of dividend is the least common type compared to stock or cash dividends. This type of dividend becomes an option if the company doesn't have sufficient funds to allocate healthy payments. This type of dividend has a financial value even though it is always considered a nonmonetary type of dividend. How does a property dividend work? For instance, Company Indigo's board of directors resolves to issue a property dividend for its 10,000 shareholders. The asset circulated by company Indigo is worth $500 to each shareholder. The average market assessment of the assets paid out to shareholders in total is 5 million dollars. The decision to sell or hold onto this asset is then made by each shareholder.

❖ Liquidating dividend: This is the act of distributing cash to shareholders with the intention of shutting down the business organization. This type of dividend is issued out after all creditor and lender obligations have been completely resolved. The dividend payout is always one of the last actions taken before the business folds up.

How do companies pay dividends?

Companies decide to pay dividends out of their present year's surplus as well as the previous year's profit after regulating depreciation and loss which has been amassed over the years. Dividends are often paid out through the method of a dividend check or the issuance of extra shares of stock. The regular practice for the payment of dividends comes in form of a check which is often sent through a mail few days after the former dividend date, the particular date on which the stock starts trading without the formerly declared date. The issuance of extra shares of stock is sometimes used instead of the use of check by individual companies and mutual funds. One thing you need to know is that dividends are taxed regardless of the form in which they are paid.

DRIP (Dividend reinvestment plan) is really beneficial to investors. If an investor prefers adding to the existing equity he or she holds, with any extra funds from the payment of dividends, automatic reinvestment of dividends reduces to bare bones. This process is contrary to receiving the payment of dividends in cash and then making use of this cash to purchase further shares. Dividend reinvestment plans operated by companies do not require commission since they are far better than using a broker.

Another prospective advantage is that certain companies actually offer investors the alternative to purchase further shares in cash at a certain discount. With a discount from 1-10%, including the bonus advantage of not having to pay commission fees, stockholders can get extra stock holdings at a beneficial price over other investors who procure shares in cash via a brokerage firm.

When do companies pay dividends?

The very moment a dividend is announced or declared, the shareholders will be notified through a press release and the information is often reported via important stock quoting services for easy reference. When the dividend is declared, the next thing is to set a record date; this ensures that every shareholder on record on that particular date has a right to be paid their dividends. The day after the record date is called the ex-date or the date which the stock commences trading ex-dividend. This basically means that a purchaser on ex-date is buying shares which are not eligible to receive the most current payment of dividends. The payable date of the dividend often comes a month after the record date.

On this payable date, the funds for payment are usually deposited with the Depository Trust Company (DTC). Afterward, DTC distributes this money to different brokerage firms across the world where the company shares are held by various shareholders. The beneficiary companies appropriately send cash dividends to client accounts or take the decision of processing DRIP transactions, depending on what the client wants. The type of dividend declared and the type of accounts where shares are owned by the shareholders determine the tax implications on the payment of dividends.

How to make money with dividend stocks?

One reason a lot of people go into the stock business is for the sole purpose of making money. What do I mean by this? Although a lot of people especially new investors find the idea of investing really impressive, the majority of them do not really know how to make money through dividend stocks. When dealing in stocks, one thing you need to know is the fact that you have to invest in a company that has the tendency to increase its dividends every year. Make sure you look at the dividend history of the company you want to invest in. Make sure it's a company that has set a good record for itself over the past 10-15 years. For instance, if a very healthy and financially stable company gives a dividend of $10 this year, there is a tendency that there would be an increase in the dividends if the company earns more profit in the future. However, the decision to pay or not to pay dividends is vested in the company to make. One other thing you need to know is that your dividends will definitely increase as long as you still hold the stock while your purchase price remains the same. Imagine you purchased 100 stocks of a company at the rate $200. The annual dividend for that year was $10. This means for the very first year, the dividend yield would be 5%. This is a very small yield when compared to the returns from other investments. Nevertheless, let us imagine that this company is profoundly healthy and going to escalate its dividends in the forthcoming years. One other way to make money from dividend stock is to buy at a cheap rate and wait to sell when the market value is relatively high. If you want to make money with dividends, one other thing you should do is to make research and not invest in companies that have a higher debt load than other companies. You can find this information in a company's balance sheet or its annual report. You also need to ensure a company's dividend per share isn't more than at least 80 percent of its earnings per share. Also, ensure the company's current ratio is greater than 1, this certifies the company's financial stability. After calculating your dividend yield, which is the yearly dividend divided by the existing stock price, ensure you spend really less compared to what you earn.

How to calculate a stock dividend yield?

What is a dividend yield? The dividend yield is the percentage of your investment that is being paid to you by a stock in the form of dividends. It can also be likened to an interest a stock yields. To find your dividend yield, you have to find the present price per share of the particular stock you are interested in. For publicly-traded companies, the present stock price can be found on websites of any major stock index. Examples are NASDAQ or S&P 500. Note that the share price of any company's stock fluctuates based on the company's activeness. This basically explains why certain estimations for the dividend yield of any company's stock may not be accurate if there is a sudden jolt in the stock's price. The next thing is to find the DPS value of the stock you own. The formula for finding DPS is DPS= D-SD/S. D stands for the amount of the money paid in regular dividends, SD stands for the amount paid in special, one-time dividends, while S stands for the total number of shares of company stock owned by investors. D and SD can be found on the cash flow statement of a company while S can be found on the balance sheet. Dividend yield= Dividend per share/ stock price. If dividend per share equals $1 and stock price equals $20, DY= $1/$20

DY= 0.05 = 5%.

The dividends yield here equals 5% in the above equation.

Is a high payout dividend good or bad?

What is a dividend payout ratio? The dividend payout ratio simply determines the ratio of the entire amount of dividends disbursed to shareholders relative to the net income of the company. It is the percentage of income given out to shareholders in the form of dividends. The company retains the amount of money which is not paid to shareholders to pay off debt or to reinvest in certain important operations. It is sometimes simply referred to as the payout ratio. The dividend payout ratio often specifies how much a company has to return to its shareholders against how much the company decides to reinvest or pay off debts. You can calculate this dividends payout ratio by dividing the dividend per share by the earnings per share or simply the division of dividends by net income. The question now is "how do we know when a company's payout ratio is good or bad?" Companies that do not pay dividends have a payout ratio of 0% as well as companies that are fond of paying out their entire net income as dividends. When a company's payout ratio is over 100% on the other hand, it simply means such company is giving out more than it earns as dividends, which is not really a good sign as such company might be forced to stop paying dividends altogether. When a company's payout ratio is on a steady leap, it may be a good sign that such company is on its verge of maturity and a healthy one to invest in However, when a company's payout ratio takes a huge leap, it could be a warning sign that such company is running into debt or going to end up becoming unsustainable.

Profiting for the long term through compounding

In the world of investing, one way to grow your money faster and easier is to invest your earnings along with your initial capital. This act is known as compounding. Here's how the rule of compounding works:

Compound interest will definitely help make an accelerated rate of income when compared to the simple interest which is only calculated on the principal amount. What compound interest also stands for is the fact that you simply earn more money on your interest income which results in an escalating amount of money for you. Albert Einstein once illustrated that the most influential force in the universe was the standard of compounding. In investing, this demonstrates itself through a term known as compound interest.

For better illustration, imagine you have a sum of $500 and earn 10% in interest. This amounts to a total of $550. Now if you earn an interest of 10% on your initial $550, you end up with $605. This continues until you have a very huge sum of money. This is exactly how a lot of people have profited from the theory of compound interest.

This also explains the reason for the achievement of every individual on the Forbes 400 list, and virtually any other human can reap from the amazing benefits of compounding when they invest in the right way. Benjamin Franklin was noted and popular for explaining how the theory of compound interest happens to be the best way to make real money on time. The theory of compound interest is highly convincing and very fast when it comes to making the best of your investments. One beautiful thing everyone should know about the compound interest is the fact that the amount you can save every month is really important. The amount of time you choose to invest in your plan also matters so much. The sooner you learn the act of compounding, the better the knowledge you will have.

Chapter 3

STOCK MARKET LANGUAGE & TERMINOLOGIES

Every field has its own "terms" and "language" which have been specially designed and cannot be used outside the field it was originally designed for. Just as the field of law has its own words and terminologies which would never make sense if used in other fields or context, the field of technology also has its own set of words and language. Similarly, the stock market also has its own special language and terminologies. Some of these terms have been compiled in this chapter to help you get familiar with their meanings and how to use such words perfectly. Some of these terminologies are listed below:

❖ **ADVANCED COMPANIES:** An advanced company can be defined as an issuer which is listed on Canada's TSX enterprise exchange who ensures the gratification of the exchange's Tier-one listing criteria. In case you are curious about what Tier one means, it is basically the exchange's primary tier. Only companies with the most substantial and noteworthy financial resources have the right to become members of this tier. These Companies may function in various fields ranging from mining, oil and gas, mixed industry, technology, life sciences, real estate, or investment. The status of Tier-one offers companies entry to a more encouraging supervisory environment, diminished filling requirements, and better prospect for participation by institutional investors. While the purpose of TSX venture exchange is explicitly developing/ unindustrialized companies seeking venture capital, advanced companies have directors who have recognized regulations and the companies in question must have substantial financial assets at their disposal.

❖ **AGENT:** An agent in authorized terms can be defined as an individual who has been given legal rights to perform certain roles on behalf of another individual or body. An agent may be hired to take the place of a client in negotiations and other transactions with third parties. The agent may be given decision-making authority. Several people use a special agent from time to time. Such agents include a real estate agent, an insurance agent, or travel agents. Two common types of these agents are attorneys who represent their clients in legal affairs and stockbrokers who are appointed by investors to make investment decisions on their behalf. The person who is epitomized by this agent is known as the principal. In finance, it denotes a fiduciary relationship, in which an agent is accredited to implement transactions on behalf of the client. Most people hire agents to perform tasks that they lack the time or expertise to do for themselves. Investors employ stockbrokers to act as middlemen between them and the stock market. More commonly, potential landowners use agents as middlemen, depending on the specialist's greater skills and negotiation. Businesses also hire agents to take their place in a specific venture or negotiation relying on the agents' loftier skills, contacts, or contextual information to seal deals.

❖ **ALL OR NONE ORDER:** This is an order to purchase or trade a stock that must be implemented in its totality or not implemented at all. AON orders that cannot be implemented instantly often continue being active until they are implemented or annulled. It can also be defined as a command used on a buy or sell order that inculcates the broker to fill the order completely or not at all. For instance, if there are too few shares to fill the order exclusively, the order is disproved when the market closes. An AON order is considered a duration or an interval order because the trader gives instructions to the broker concerning how the order has to be filled which determines how long the order remains active.

❖ **ARBITRAGE:** This refers to acquiring and vending similar security at the same time in diverse markets to take advantage of a price difference between the two distinct markets. In a market arbitrage trade, an arbitrageur would short-sell the higher priced one. The profit is the range between the two properties. This practice takes its roots firmly in the postulation that an asset that is merchandised worldwide is priced contrarily in various markets. That is, the equivalent stock may have a market value in Europe that is totally different from its value on the New York Stock exchange. In principle, the amounts of the same asset on both exchanges should be one and the same at all times, but market arbitrage opportunities ascend when they are not. Market arbitrage is a careless activity in the sense that traders are solely buying and selling equivalent amounts of the same assets at the same time. This is why arbitrage is often called "reckless profit".

❖ **ASSETS:** An asset is defined as anything which is tangible or a resource of value that can be changed into cash. Assets can be owned by individuals, companies, and governments. For a corporation, an asset might produce revenue or benefit from using or possessing an asset. Examples of these assets include cash and cash equivalents, certificate of deposit, checking and savings accounts, money market accounts, physical cash, and treasury bills. Property or land can also be considered an asset as well as household furnishings, jewelry, vehicles annuities, bonds, the cash value of life insurance policies, mutual funds, etc. An individual's net worth is often calculated when his or her legal responsibility or liabilities are deducted from assets. In other words, your assets are basically all that belongs to you while liabilities are the things you owe.

❖ **ALBERTA SECURITIES COMMISSION:**
This is a supervisory organization which manages and imposes securities legislation in the Canadian province of Alberta. Their main purposes are to foster fair and efficient capital markets in Alberta and to protect investors. The ASC, as it is commonly known, is an affiliate of the Canadian Securities Administrators, the charitable canopy organization of Canada's provincial and territorial securities regulators.

❖ **BASIS POINT:** Basis point can be defined as a common unit of quantity for interest rates and other percentages in finance. One basis point is equivalent to one over hundredth of one percent. $1/100^{th}$ of 1% or 0.0001, and can be used to represent the percentage modification in a financial mechanism. The connection between percentage changes and the basis points can be concise as follows: 1% change= 100 basis points and 0.01% = 1 basis point. The basis point originates from the base move amongst two percentages, or the range between two interest rates. Because the fluctuations documented are commonly constricted, and because trivial changes can have massive results, the basis is a segment of a percent. The basis point is universally used for calculating fluctuations in interest rates, equity indices, and the yield of a fixed revenue safety or security. Bonds and loans are often quoted in basis point terms.

❖ **BEAR MARKET:** This is a situation in which securities prices fall 20% or more from topical inflations amid prevalent disapproval and negative investor sentiment. Stereotypically bear markets are connected with debilities in an inclusive market or index like the S&P 500, but singular securities or commodities can be considered to be in a bear market if they go through a decline of 20% or extra over a continuous period of time- commonly a couple of months or more. Bear markets can last for numerous years or just a number of weeks. A profane bear market can actually last anywhere from 10-20 years and is often categorized below average returns on a constant basis. There may be demonstrations surrounding secular bear markets where stocks or indexes rally for a particular time, but the achievements are not sustained and prices relapse to lower levels.

❖ **BEST EFFORTS UNDERWRITING:** This is a prescribed term in which an underwriter gives a promise to make their paramount effort to trade as much of a security contribution (e.g., IPO) as probable. Best-effort agreements are used principally for securities in a less than perfect market circumstance or with advanced risks, such as an unseasoned offering. Best efforts release underwriters from being responsible for any portfolio of shares they are not able to sell. The underwriter does not give a warranty that it will sell the whole IPO issue in a best-efforts settlement. A best-effort contract restricts both the underwriter's risk and the underwriter's earnings since they accept a flat fee for their services.

❖ **BALANCE SHEET:** A balance sheet can be defined as a financial statement that summarizes a company's assets and liabilities plus owner's equity. The balance sheet refers to a specific time. This particular time is typically the end of a quarter, half-year or year. Individuals, establishments, aids, and many other entities make use of balance sheets. The owner's equity basically refers to the shareholders' investment minus the company extractions plus the net income since the company commenced. The balance sheet is otherwise known as the statement of financial position. The owner's equity is also the same as the stockholder's equity or shareholder equity. The balance sheet is one of the foremost financial statement used by accountants. The balance sheet gives an account of what a company's financial position is on a specified date. In fact, a lot of people consider it a snapshot of the firm's financial position at a particular time. Concerned parties such as creditors can perceive what belongs to an entity as well as the liabilities a business has on a specific date. In other words, they recognize what the firm's financial position is at a particular time. A bank uses the statistics in a balance sheet to decide whether to lend a loan aspirant money. The bank might also use it to make decisions about lending a borrower more money. Furthermore, a corporation's management, stakeholders, competitors, and merchants all strive to scrutinize a firm's balance sheet. For instance, before bearing in mind whether to offer credit terms, a supplier needs to be able to tell what exactly the financial stand of the buyer is. Some consumers, Trade unions, and government organizations may also want to know the state of a company's balance sheet. The budgetary aggregate of the whole thing on the left of a balance sheet must be identical to the aggregate on the right. There must be a 'balance'.

❖ **BLACK SCHOLES MARKET:** Black-Scholes is an evaluating approach used to define the reasonable value of hypothetical value for a call or a put alternative based on six variables such as impulsiveness, type of preference, fundamental stock price, time, strike price and risk-free rate. The significance of assumption is more in case of stock market offshoots, and hence appropriate pricing of options eliminates the chance for any arbitrage. There are two essential models for option pricing –Binomial model and the Black-Scholes Model. The model is used to regulate the price of a European Call selection, which fundamentally means that the option can be implemented on the termination date.

❖ **BULL MARKET:** This is the situation of a commercial market of a cluster of securities in which prices are escalating or are anticipated to increase. This term is most often used to refer to the stock market but can be used to refer to anything that is traded, such as bonds, real estates, currencies, and commodities. Because prices of securities rise and fall fundamentally incessantly during trading, the word "bull market" is classically set aside for prolonged periods in which a great quota of security values are escalating. Bull markets are inclined to last for several months or even years. Bull markets are categorized by positivity, investor assurance, and prospects that strong outcomes should linger for an extended period of time. It is challenging to forecast unswervingly when the trends in the market might change. Part of the difficulty is that psychological effects and speculation may sometimes play a huge role in the markets.

❖ **BUSINESS TRUST:** This is a kind of fiduciary relationship whereby a particular party often referred to as the trustor, confers unto another party (the trustee) the right to hold title to certain property or assets for the advantage or benefit of a third party, who is known as the beneficiary.

❖ **BLUE CHIP:** A blue chip can be defined as the stock of a huge perfectly recognized and financially comprehensive company that has functioned for several years. A blue-chip stock usually has a market capitalization in the billions, is commonly the market front-runner, or among the top three corporations in its sector. A blue-chip stock is more often than not a domestic name. Some examples of blue-chip stocks include IBM Corp, Coca-Cola Co., and Boeing Co. While the payment of dividends isn't categorically compulsory for a stock to be considered a blue-chip, majority of blue chips actually have an extensive record of paying steady or rising dividends. The term is assumed to have been derived from poker, where blue chips happen to be the most luxurious chips. A blue-chip stock is, in general, a section of the most trustworthy market indexes or averages such as the DOW JONES Industrial Average, S&P 500, and the Nasdaq 100 in the U.S, the TSX 60 in Canada, or the FTSE index in the U.K.

A company doesn't necessarily need to be big to a certain extent to attain the blue-chip status. A commonly acknowledged yardstick is a market capitalization of $5 billion, while market or sector leaders can be establishments of all dimensions. Although most blue-chip corporations have endured several trials and market cycles, which has led to them being observed as a conducive investment, this doesn't necessarily mean every blue-chip company has the same standard.

❖ **BROKER:** A stockbroker is an expert who implements buy and sell orders for stocks and supplementary securities on behalf of clients. A stockbroker is also the same as a registered representative, investment adviser, or solely broker. A broker is frequently connected with a brokerage firm and takes care of transactions for marketing and institutional customers alike. Stockbrokers often get commissions for the services they render but the individual reward can differ greatly depending on where they work. Brokerage firms and broker-dealers are also sometimes called stockbrokers themselves. Discount brokers happen to be the most sought after and generally referenced stockbroker firms. Ability to purchase and sell stocks and other securities necessitate entrance to one of the key exchanges such as the New York stock exchange (NYSE) or the NASDAQ. To trade on these particular transactions or exchanges, you have to be a member of the exchange or fit into a member firm. Member partnerships and many of the people who work for them are registered as brokers or broker-dealers by FINRA. While you may buy stock shares directly from the business that distributes them, it is more stress-free to work with a stockbroker. Back in the days, getting access to the stock market was far more expensive and as a result, it was only lucrative for great net-worth investors. These investors would stereotypically work with a full-service broker and pay tons of money for implementing a trade. Nevertheless, the upsurge of the internet and successive improvements in technology paved the way for discount brokers to make available less expensive, faster, and more mechanized access to interactions. This has permitted investors to trade the stock markets with smaller transaction fees, making it reasonable to invest and trade unfluctuating with much smaller-sized accounts. So much so that the mainstream of accounts in the market are held with discount brokers.

❖ **BOOK VALUE:** This refers to the entire amount, the value of a corporation would be if it discharged its assets and refunded its entire liabilities. Book value may also represent the worth of a specific asset on the establishment's balance sheet after taking accrued devaluation into account. Book value is calculated by taking a company's fixed assets (which includes land, buildings, computers, etc.) and deducting out insubstantial assets (such as patents) and liabilities – including preferred stock, debt, and accounts payable. The worth you have left after this calculation signifies what the firm is fundamentally worth. Since book value embodies the fundamental net worth of a corporation, it is a very useful tool for investors who want to know if a corporation is understated or exorbitant, which could specify a prospective time to purchase or sell. For instance, value investors hunt for companies dealing in prices at or lower than book value (which specifies a price-book ratio or less than 1.0) which suggests the shares are being traded for less than the company's real value.

❖ **CAPITAL GAIN:** This is an escalation in the worth of a capital asset (investment or real estate) that gives it a sophisticated worth than the purchase price. The profit is not comprehended until the asset is traded. A capital gain may be temporary (a year or less) or long-term (more than a year) and must be requested on income taxes. While capital gains are commonly accompanied with stocks and funds due to their intrinsic price unpredictability, a capital gain can happen in any security that is traded for a price greater than the price it was originally purchased. Realized capital gains actually occur when an asset is sold, which activates a taxable event. Unrealized gains and losses, sometimes referred to as paper gains or losses, replicate an escalation or reduction in investment's value but have not yet prompted a taxable incident.

❖ **CAPITAL STOCK:** The capital stock is the amount of common and chosen shares that a corporation is sanctioned to issue, according to its commercial charter. The quantity acknowledged by the establishment when it gave out shares of its capital stock is recounted in the shareholders' equity segment of the balance sheet. Companies can give out additional capital stock ultimately or buy back shares that are presently owned by shareholders. Capital stock can only be issued or given out by the corporation, and it is the supreme number of shares that can ever be unresolved. It is a means by which a corporation can get capital to develop its business. The stock given can be purchased by investors, who try to find price increase and dividends or substituted for assets, like equipment required for running their business. The exact number of outstanding shares which are shares issued to investors is not automatically equal to the number of available or accredited shares issued by the firm. A corporation can transform this number by voting to rectify its charter which often implies that they want to issue stock to earn or get additional capital.

CAPITAL STOCK= Number of shares issued × per value per share.

❖ CAPITALIZATION CHANGE:

Capitalization change refers to a variation of a company's capital arrangement which includes both equity and debt. A company's primary capitalization encompasses equity and possibly some debt. When there's a transformation to equity or both modules, (if the debt is part of the capital structure), a capitalization alters results. Generally, a company commences its lifespan with capital donated by the originators, family, and friends. As the company develops, it may look for funds from venture Wealth investors. Any new capital introduced into the company will lead to a capitalization change- basically, a larger quantity of equity at this point. Supposing that this corporation would then be in a situation to search for bank loans or even issue debt. The accumulation of debt to the balance sheet would signify additional capitalization transformation. As the establishment keeps growing into maturity, its funding needs become more refined, calling for several modifications, even alterations depending on the development of the firm and the changing aspects of the industry, to the capital organization. The issuance of innovative shares and supposition of debt for a large achievement, for illustration, could primarily modify the capitalization of a firm. An accountable company endeavors to steady the amount of equity and debt in its capital structure in accordance with its needs. Issuing equity is luxurious and dilutive; debt funding is less expensive and generates tax shields, but too much debt exposes a firm to greater risk. A firm that modifies its capital structure hypothetically must keep the welfare of its shareholders' in mind, but it should lessen the monetary danger to the enterprise. A set of methods of this type of risk is the capitalization of ratio, the amount of debt in the capital structure. The three variants of the capitalization ratio are debt-equity, lasting debt-to-capitalization and entire debt-to- capitalization. What is realistic in terms of the capitalization ratio is determined by the industry and the future predictions for the firm. A company, for example, could have a moderately high ratio unlike its peers, but stronger near-term productivity dimensions to pay down dues to decrease the ratio to a convenient level.

❖ **DISCLOSURE:** In the financial domain, disclosure ultimately refers to the act of letting out all pertinent information on a corporation that may impact investment decision-making. Both optimistic and destructive news, statistics, and other information about its procedures that affect its actions, in a timely manner. Just like disclosure in the law, the idea is that, in the interest of justice, all parties should have equivalent access to a similar set of truths. Although regulation of business had been in existence all along, the federal government-authorized disclosure came into existence in the United States along with the passage of the Securities Act of 1933 together with the Securities Exchange Act of 1934. The two acts were responses to the stock market Crash of 1929 and the succeeding Great Depression. The members of the public and the political candidates alike censured a lack of pellucidity in commercial operations for escalating –if not outright causing- the financial disaster. Since then, supplementary legislation, such as the Sarbanes-Oxley Act of 2002, has prolonged public company disclosure requirements.

❖ **CANADIAN DEPOSITORY FOR SECURITIES LIMITED (CDS):** The Canadian depository for securities limited is Canada's nationwide securities store, clearing and reimbursement hub. It delivers dependable and economical depository, clearing and settlement services to members in Canada's equity, fixed revenue, and currency markets. The duties of this body include the benign custody and association of securities, post-trade dealings dispensation, precise record-keeping and the assortment and circulation of securities entitlements such as dividends and interest payments. CDS is controlled by the securities commission of Ontario and Quebec and the bank of Canada. CDS amalgamated in June 1970, in answer to increasing costs for back-office purposes and improved trading capacities in Canadian Capital markets. It handled roughly 6,000 day-to-day exchange trades in its original year. Today, as a subordinate of TMX Collection, CDS takes care of more than 1.6 million daily national and cross-border securities trades and supervisions over $4 trillion of securities. TMX Collection functions and handles exchanges across asset classes, which includes the Toronto and Montreal exchanges. As the parent corporation has added competencies through procurement, CDS has continued to be the chief benefactor of equities and fixed revenue reimbursement and trade settlement services. CDS provided the trading substructure and technology that permitted the Canadian Capital Markets Association (CCMA) to executive T+2 initiative in 2017 that reduced trade defrayals of investment funds, equities, and bonds from three to two business days.

- ❖ **CLOSED-END INVESTMENT FUND:** A closed-end fund is a combined investment model founded on issuing a fixed number of shares which are not convertible from the fund. Unlike open funds, new shares in a closed-end fund are not generated by managers to meet ultimatum from stockholders. Instead, the shares can be procured and sold only in the market which is the innovative design of the mutual fund, which precedes open-end mutual funds but compromises the same vigorously achieved pooled investments. Closed-end funds are typically listed on a documented stock exchange and can be accepted and sold on that exchange. The price per share depends solely on the type of market and is frequently unlike the fundamental value or net asset value (NAV) per share of the savings held by the account. The price is said to be at a discount or premium to the NAV when it is below or above the NAV, correspondingly.

❖ **TICKER SYMBOL**: Ticker symbol or stock symbol is a contraction which is often used for the unique identification of widely merchandized shares of a specific stock on a certain stock market. A stock symbol may be a combination of letters and numbers or in form of any of these two. "Ticker symbol" refers to the signs that were written on the ticker tape of a ticker tape appliance. A ticker symbol can also be defined as an organization of characters—

typically letters which actually represent specific securities registered on an exchange or otherwise traded publicly. When security is issued by a company to the public marketplace, an available ticker symbol is often selected for its securities that investors and dealers use to manage orders. Every registered security has an exclusive ticker symbol, which facilitates the enormous collection of trade orders that flow through the monetary markets daily. Standard & Poor's (S&P) industrialized the contemporary ticker which is only in the form of letters in the United States to standardize investing. Formerly, a solitary firm could have several ticker symbols among various individual stock markets. The term "ticker" refers to the sound which the tape machines produce, which were one time prevalent in usage but presently have basically been substituted by countless kinds of electronic digital tickers. Individually, the stock market has a constructing agreement which is used for the issuance of tickers precise to that stock market.

❖ **EPS:** Earnings per share (EPS) can be simply defined as a corporation's income divided by the unresolved shares of its shared or common stock. The subsequent number functions as a pointer of a corporation's productivity. It is very common for a business to account EPS that is attuned for unusual items and possible share dilution. The higher a company's EPS, the more lucrative it is considered. The EPS worth is analyzed in the form of the net worth. (It is the same as proceeds or returns) allocated through the obtainable shares. A more advanced calculation regulates the numerator and denominator for shares that could be shaped via alternatives, alterable dues, or permits. You should always consider the numerator if it is familiar for on-going operations.

To determine a business's EPS, the balance sheet and income statement are often used to discover the period-end amount of common shares, dividends paid on preferred stock (if any), and the net income or remunerations. It is more precise to use a subjective regular number of joint shares over the reporting term because the number of shares can alter over time.

Any stock dividends or splits that happen must be replicated in the calculation of the slanted average number of shares unresolved. Several databases abridge the calculation by making use of the number of shares unresolved at the conclusion of an era.

The earnings-per-share metric is one of the most significant variables in shaping a share's price. It is also a key factor used to calculate the price-to-earnings (P/E) valuation ratio, where the E in P/E refers to EPS. By dividing a business's share price by its earnings per share, a stakeholder is able to see the worth of a stock in terms of how much the market is eager to pay for each dollar of earnings. EPS is one of the voluminous indicators you could use to select stocks. If you are interested in understanding, your subsequent step is to select a broker that suits your investment style. Relating EPS in complete terms may not have much significance to investors since regular shareholders do not have straight access to the earnings. As a substitute, stockholders will liken EPS with the share price of the stock to regulate the value of earnings and how investors feel about forthcoming development.

❖ **IPO:** IPO can be defined as a form of public contribution in which shares of a company are sold to institutional investors and regularly also retail (individual) investors; an IPO is recognized by one or more asset banks, who also position for the listing of the shares on single or multiple exchanges of stock. The medium used is colloquially known as floating or going public, a confidentially-held company is converted into a public company. Initial public offerings can be used to nurture new equity capital for the company in concern, to make money from the investments made by private stockholders including pioneers of companies or individual shareholders as well as to facilitate stress-free trading of prevailing holdings or imminent principal raising by transforming into well-known establishments. Subsequently, stocks transacted without restrictions in the open market are identified as the free float. Stock exchanges specify a least free float both in total relations (the entire worth which is regulated by the stock rate increased by the quantity of stocks traded out to the members of the public) also in the form of an amount of the entire share capital (i.e., the number of shares sold to the public divided by the total shares unresolved). Although IPO offers many reimbursements, there are also noteworthy costs involved, chiefly those related with the procedure such as banking and legal fees, as well as the ongoing obligation to reveal vital and sometimes delicate information. Specifics of the projected offering are divulged to prospective procurers in the form of a long document which is referred to as a prospectus. Most corporations assume an IPO with the help of an investment banking firm substituting the capacity of an underwriter. Underwriters are known for providing various services which include helping with appropriately evaluating the worth of shares (share price) and launching a public market for shares (initial sale). Substitute methods such as the Dutch auction have also been discovered and used for numerous IPOs.

❖ **CFD:** CFD is simply an acronym for the term "contract for difference" A contract for difference (CFD) is basically a general form of imitative trading. CFD trading permits you to take risks on the increasing or dwindling prices of fast-moving world-wide monetary markets (or instruments) such as shares, indices, commodities, currencies, and treasuries. The contract for difference (CFD) gives several European traders and investors a chance to profit from price fluctuations without possessing the fundamental asset. It's a comparatively humble security which is calculated by the asset's movement between trade access and departure, totaling only the price alteration without deliberation of the asset's fundamental value. This is proficient through a deal between client and broker and does not apply any stock, forex, commodity, or futures exchange. Trading CFDs give you several major compensations that have augmented the instruments' colossal popularity in the past era. One particular question a lot of people tend to ask about CFD is "How does a CFD Work?" Now, I will give a breakdown of what the CFD looks like. Let's assume a share actually has a standard price of $25.26 when the dealer purchases 100 shares, the charge of the transaction is $2,526 including commission and fees. This trade necessitates at least $1,263 in acceptable or unrestricted currency at an outdated dealer in a 50% border transaction, whereas a CFD agent previously asked for only a 5% border, or $126.30. A CFD transaction will replicate a forfeiture equivalent to the magnitude of the range at the interval of the transaction, therefore, if the spread is 5 cents, there is a need for an increase of 5 cents for the point to hit the breakeven price. You'll realize a 5-cent gain if you retained the stock absolutely but would have been required to pay a commission and acquired a loftier capital expenditure. If the stock marches to an offer or an auction price of $25.76 in a traditional broker account, it can be traded for a $50 increase or $50/$1263=3.95% earnings. However, when the nation-wide exchange reaches this price, the CFD bid price may only be $25.74. The CFD profit will be lesser because the dealer must depart at the bid price and the spread is greater than on the steady market. In this example, the CFD trader earns a projected $48 or $48/$126.30=38% reoccurrence on investment. The CFD broker may also need the trader to purchase at a sophisticated original price, $25.28 for example. Even so, the $46 to $48 earned on the CFD trade represents a net profit, while the $50 profit from possessing the stock outright doesn't consist of commissions or supplementary fees, giving more money to the CFD dealer.

- ❖ **MUTUAL FUNDS:** What are mutual funds? A mutual fund is a kind of financial instrument which consists of a pool of money gotten from a number of investors to capitalize in securities such as stocks, bonds, money market instruments, and other possessions. Mutual funds are controlled and activated by qualified money managers, who distribute the account's assets and endeavor to produce capital gains or revenue for the fund's stockholders. A mutual fund's assortment is designed and upheld to equal the investment goals stated in its brochure. What a mutual fund does is to help in pooling money from the investing public and use that money to purchase additional securities, typically stocks and bonds. The worth of the mutual fund establishment is influenced by the presentation of the securities it chooses to purchase. Therefore, when you succeed in acquiring a unit or share of a mutual fund, you are purchasing the enactment of its assortment or more specifically, a fragment of the portfolio's worth. Taking the risk to invest in a share of a mutual fund is not the same with investing in shares of stock. Unlike stock, mutual fund shares do not allow its holders any voting privileges.   One thing you should understand is, a share of a mutual fund signifies investments in numerous different stocks (or other securities) as an alternative of just one holding. The regular mutual fund holds hundreds of diverse securities, which basically means mutual fund shareholders benefit vital modification at a little price. Take into consideration an investor who purchases only

Google stock earlier before the corporation has a bad quarter. He stands a chance of losing a countless deal of value simply because he has laid all his eggs in a basket and also has all his money tied in a firm. On the other hand, an entirely different investor may purchase shares of a mutual fund that happens to possess some Google stock. When Google has a bad quarter, she only throws away a fraction as much because Google is just a minor part of the fund's portfolio. How does a mutual fund Work? A mutual fund is equally an asset and an authentic corporation. This double nature may appear bizarre, but it is in no way different from how a share of AAPL is a depiction of Apple, Inc. When an investor purchases Apple stock, he is purchasing portion ownership of the establishment and its assets. Correspondingly, a mutual fund investor is purchasing part ownership of the mutual fund corporation and its possessions. The dissimilarity is that Apple is concerned with the production of smartphones while mutual fund company specializes in investment making. Investors characteristically make a return from a mutual fund in three ways. Revenue is gotten from dividends on stocks and interests on bonds retained in the fund's collection. A fund reimburses nearly all of the income it gets over the year to pay owners in the system of distribution. Funds usually offer investors an ultimatum either to be given a check for distributions or to plow the earnings and acquire more shares. If the fund trades securities that have augmented in price, the fund takes a capital gain. A lot of these funds also authorize these gains to investors in a distribution. If fund holdings upsurge in price but are not traded by the fund manager, the fund's shares rise in price. You can then trade your mutual fund shares for a turnover in the market. If a mutual fund is interpreted as a cybernetic company, its CEO is the fund manager, occasionally called its asset adviser. The fund manager is employed by a board of directors and is lawfully obliged to work in the best attention of mutual fund shareholders. Most fund managers are also owners of the fund. There are very rare other employees in a mutual fund corporation. The investment adviser or fund manager may hire the service of some other analysts to help with the selection of investments or performance of market investigation. A fund accountant is retained on staff to compute the fund's NAV, the day-to-day worth of the portfolio that regulates if share prices increase or reduce. Mutual funds should also have a compliance officer or two, and perhaps an attorney, to keep up with government principles.

❖ **Equity shares:** Equity shares are the foremost basis of finance of an establishment. They are allotted to the entire members of the general public. Equity shareholders do not relish any superior rights with respect to reimbursement of wealth and dividend. They are eligible to enduring income of the company, but these people have the luxury of controlling the matters of the business and all the shareholders co-operatively are the owners of the company. Equity shares are the shares of joint stock companies which is given out to the members of the public as the core source of durable financing. The only reason it's known as long-term funding is that equity shares are officially not convertible naturally. The worth of equity share is quantified in expressions of the appearance cost of an individual stock, which is otherwise known as the issue worth, respective worth, book value, or market worth. Typically, the asset's value minus liabilities give us the asset's equity value. To curtail this to an equation for bookkeeping purposes, it's Assets-Liabilities=Equity. Equity as a Share of Proprietorship. The term equity has more than one likely meaning, depending on how it's used. For example, in the monetary sense, equity defines how much of an asset each person possesses after all arrears have been funded and liabilities are deducted. Another term used with this kind of financial equity is preference. Preference specifies which shareholders get remunerated first, even if the company files liquidation. Over-all equity shareholders have the benefit of voting privileges, though, and preference shareholders don't get to vote.

❖ **Yield:** This can be defined as the per ratio of a share divided by the price per share. In other words, it can be defined as an establishment's entire yearly- payment of dividends divided by the market capitalization, supposing the number of shares is persistent. It is often conveyed as a percentage.

The dividend yield is used to analyze the receiving on investment (shares) bearing in mind only the proceeds in the form of aggregate dividends acknowledged by the company all through the year.

❖ **What is a Growth Stock:** A growth stock can be defined as a share in a corporation that is predicted to develop at a frequency meaningfully above the usual for the market. These stocks commonly are not known for paying dividends, as the enterprises usually want to plow any earnings in order to hasten growth in the diminutive term. Investors then earn money through revenue allocation when their shares are sold out ultimately. Investment in growth stocks can be unsafe because they do not pay dividends. However, the only chance an investor has to make money on their investment is when they eventually trade their shares. If the company does not do well, investors take a forfeiture on the stock when the time comes to trade it. Today, growth stocks constitute a variety of knowledge, biotech, and some customer unrestricted business. Growth stocks incline to share some little collective traits. For example, growth corporations tend to have exclusive product ranks. They may hold copyrights or access to know-how that put them ahead of others in their business. In order to stay ahead of opponents, they plow profits to improve even newer skills and exclusive rights as a way to safeguard longer term progress. Because of their modernization, they often have a very reliable consumer base or a noteworthy amount of market stake in their business. For instance, an app development corporation that is the first to deliver a new facility may be a growth stock, because it increases market share by being the first company to deliver a new service. If other app corporations arrive in the market with their own varieties of the service, the company that succeeds to entice and hold the principal number of users may become a growth stock. Many small-cap stocks are well thought-out growth stocks. Nevertheless, some superior companies also issue growth stocks.

❖ **SHAREHOLDER**: A shareholder is also known as a **stockholder**; this could be an individual, establishment, organization, or administration that possesses at least one share in a firm. This comprises both corporations listed in a stock exchange and unlisted ones. By holding stocks, a shareholder keeps a percentage of that company. The stockholders are the proprietors of the company – the ones to whom the business is accountable for the business that it does. As well as proprietorship, stockholders have the authority to declare dividends, they can elect who may sit on the board of directors and have a contribution in the business's strategy and purposes. Proprietors of shares in listed companies also have the right to trade their shares at any time they want. Shareholders are not individually accountable for the corporation's responsibilities and amount overdue – the only cash they risk is what they paid when they acquired the shares. This shouldn't be confused with partnerships or sole proprietorships.

Chapter 4

How to find & choose a good stock

Most new investors are often conflicted in this area. "How do I find and choose a good stock?" This chapter will answer every question you probably have on your mind in this aspect. Ranging from the things to look for in a company you wish to invest in to warning signs you need to study before putting your money in a company. Another important thing you need is the right way to go about diversifying your income while investing. The cliché "do not have all your eggs in one basket" is truly relevant here.

Although there isn't a specific method in selecting and finding a good stock, there are several ways to go about your stock selection but smart investors have their own methods that have paid off over the years. You can also adopt any of these methods as well and might end up becoming an inspiration to several others who are interested in investing as well. Selecting a good stock can be a very difficult thing. However, do not be discouraged, it is an exciting task as well. For me, it is exciting. The process of making your research and trusting your funds with a company with an amazing reputation is an exciting one for me.

In evaluating investments such as stock, investors actually put into consideration the stock's assessment, tactic, policies for modification, and great enthusiasm for risk. Stocks are evaluated in numerous ways, and most of the common evaluating sticks can be found on the internet or in several prints.

The most rudimentary quantity of a stock's value includes what the company pays or what the company actually earns. When you make the move to purchase or acquire a stock, you need to understand that you are buying a part of the company, so productivity is an essential concern. Imagine buying a store. It takes a while deciding on the exact amount you need to spend. Before this happens, you want to find out how much cash that store gets or earns. If the store earns quite a lot of money, you'll have to put in more money to obtain it. Now envisage dividing this store in question into a thousand proprietorship pieces. These pieces are comparable to stock shares, in the sense that you are acquiring a piece of the commercial, rather than the entire company. This explains how stocks are bought and the illustration here is given to make you understand the technical idea in a basic form.

You can be paid by the business for your proprietorship stake in numerous ways. A portion of the profit may be allocated to you by the company, which for shareholders actually comes in the method of a sporadic or periodic dividend. The business can choose to keep expanding the business while plowing money gotten to grow profitability and advance the general worth of the industry. In cases like this, a more prized business makes each piece, or share, of the business more treasured. In such a situation, the more valued share intrinsically worth an advanced price, giving the share's owner capital increase, also known as a rising or escalating stock price.

Like I said earlier, you need to understand that it isn't all companies that pay dividends. As a matter of fact, several fast-growing corporations choose to plow their cash rather than pay out a dividend. Great, securer firms are more probable to pay a dividend than are their lesser, more unpredictable counterparts.

The maximum degree for stocks is the price to earnings ratio, known as the P/E. This ratio which is actually accessible in stock tables takes the share price and splits it by a business's yearly net income. So a stock exchange for $20 and swaggering yearly net income of $2 a share would have a price/earnings ratio, or P/E, of 10. Market experts actually disagree about what establishes a low-priced or luxurious stock. Factually, stocks have averaged a P/E in the mid-teens, though, in topical years, the market P/E has been advanced, often closer to 20. As a universal rule of thumb, stocks with P/Es advanced than the broader market P/E are well-thought-out exclusive, while stocks with a below-market P/E are reflected inexpensive.

But you need to keep in mind that P/E's aren't an impeccable yardstick. A corporation that is lesser and rising fast may have a very high P/E, since it may make pintsize but has a great stock price. If a quality growth rate can actually be permanently maintained, and rapidly grow its incomes, a stock that appears exclusive on a P/E basis can quickly seem like a giveaway. Equally, a corporation may have a low P/E because its stock has been smashed in expectation of meager future income. Thus, what appears to be a really "discounted" stock may be cheap because so many people have come to the conclusion that it's indeed a terrible investment. Such an alluringly low P/E related to a bad business is called a "worth or value trap."

Other general methods comprise the dividend yield, price-to-book and, at times, price-to-sales. These are modest ratios that scrutinize the stock price against the subsequent figure, and these procedures can also be effortlessly found by reviewing stock tables.

Investors pursuing healthier value try to find stocks paying sophisticated yields than the general market, but that's just one deliberation for an investor when determining whether or not to procure a stock. So many people have been really conflicted in this area. The apprehension of "not knowing" what to expect and the fear of being scammed actually put so many people on edge.

Selection of stocks is much like assessing any company you might consider purchasing. After all, when you purchase a stock, you're fundamentally acquiring a stake in a business.

Selecting the accurate firm to invest in may appear to be the first or paramount step in constructing a portfolio, but pecuniary consultants say that an investor who is just starting out, shouldn't essentially "commence" with individual stocks. If you're just beginning to construct your investment assortment, obtaining a single stock is much dangerous and quite unsafe than purchasing a low-cost mutual fund that trails a huge group of stocks, and it's more probable that you'll realize shrill, abrupt changes in the assessment of your investment if you possess just a limited stock.

If you already have an expanded collection of mutual funds and ETFs, then you may want to enhance by including a few individual stocks. With the menace of an individual stock, there's also the chance for better revenues: The S&P 500 increased just 0.75% from 2006 through 2010; in the unchanged five years, there was an upsurge more than 348% on Apple stock. And if you happen to build your portfolio by selecting stocks manually, you'll be able to save some money, unlike an investor who pays a fund manager through the fund's expenditure ratio, to select stocks on his behalf.

Bear in mind that when you're purchasing a stock, you're becoming a share proprietor of that business. So, temporary marketplace activities on the side, the worth of your investment is actually influenced by the health of the business. This simply means that when the company you are investing in is thriving or staggering, the impact is known on your investment. Below is a list of instructions on how to choose a stock:

Buy what you are familiar with. Commence with an industry or a company that's conversant to you; the reason is to save yourself from the apprehension of not knowing what to expect. Other reasons you are advised to go for a company you are familiar with are as follows:

❖ **A place to commence:** Everyone actually has a favorite brand; some of us would rather shop a particular brand regardless of how cheap or expensive it is. When you walk into a bar, there is a drink you just wouldn't buy even if you were being paid for buying it. You alone understand why you only shop these products, or how demanding the chain restaurant down the street is on a distinctive night. That's not all the essential information, of course, but it may assist you in putting those corporations' earnings accounts in perspective.

❖ **Do away with the flimflam.** During the dot-com fizz, lots of investors fell for stocks without copiously comprehending how those companies intended to make their money. In many circumstances, it turned out, the organization didn't fully comprehend either.

What does this tell you? This simply means that you should never consider investing in a company as a result of the hype that comes with it, there are tons of people who have been misled out there, people and the internet could be misleading. All they try to do is paint you a perfect picture with sugar-coating words to make you bring your money to the intended company. Avoid this hype and only consider the future prospect of the company and exactly what the company has to offer.

❖ **Put price and assessment into consideration:** Investment experts often seek for stocks that are "low-priced" or "underestimated." Usually, what they mean is that investors are disbursing a comparatively truncated price for each buck the business makes. This is quantified by the stock's price-to-earnings ratio or P/E. (Find that quantity on SmartMoney.com, or analyze it yourself by allotting a business's share price by its net income.) Very approximately speaking, a P/E below about 15 is measured cheap, and a P/E above 20 is considered luxurious. But there's actually more to it than that, it doesn't end here.

❖ **Recognize what kind of stock you're talking about.** A corporation that's expected to develop speedily will be more luxurious than a well-known firm that's growing more slowly. Relate a firm's P/E to other corporations in the same trade to see if it's low-priced or more exclusive than its peers. This boils down to the fact that you need to do extensive research while selecting a stock to invest in. Devoting a lot of your time to research would definitely help you make a good decision.

❖ **Inexpensive isn't always decent, and luxurious isn't always a bad idea:** At times, a stock is low-priced because its business is developing less or actually decelerating. And occasionally a stock is luxurious because it's extensively anticipated to raise its earnings swiftly in the succeeding years. You want to purchase stocks that you can sensibly anticipate will be worth more later, so look at assessment combined with prospects for upcoming earnings.

- ❖ **Assess pecuniary health.** This is a very crucial step you need to consider while choosing a good stock. A lot of people have made the mistake of investing in an impecunious company; you do not want to make the same mistake as well. Start burrowing into the company's monetary reports. Do a lot of research and take note of every fault you find while doing your research. All unrestricted firms have to announce periodical and yearly reports. You can examine the Investor Dealings section of their web site, or discover certified accounts filed with the SEC on the web. Don't just lay emphasis on the most current report: What you're really considering is a reliable past of success and monetary health, not just one good quarter. Do not risk your money in a staggering company as this might pose a danger on your investment in the future. Putting this into consideration will help you find a really dependable company to invest your money in while choosing a good stock.

❖ **Look out for the company's revenue development:** No one knows what's going to happen on a daily basis, however, in the long run, stock prices upsurge when firms are building and earning more money, which typically commences with increasing revenue. You'll hear forecasters refer to income as the "top line." The revenue growth or increase of a company is a very important thing you need to consider while choosing a stock.

❖ **Find the bottom line as well:** The modification concerning revenue and expenditures is a firm's profit margin. A company that's increasing revenue while adjusting costs will also have increasing margins.

❖ **Know how much dues the corporation has:** It is very essential to know how much debt a company has before investing in it. Find out what the firm's balance sheet looks like before deciding if you would like to partner invest your money in it or not. In general terms, the share price of an establishment with extra liability is likely to be more unpredictable because more of the company's revenue has to go to interest and payment of outstanding dues. You should compare a business to its peers to perceive if it depends solely on borrowing a rare aggregate of money for its business and size. The last thing you want is to be associated with a company that has so much debt on its neck or a company that has a lot of outstanding to pay. If a company falls in this category, you should never consider being a shareowner of such a company.

- ❖ **Find a dividend.** A dividend which is usually an allocated amount of money given to shareholders on a quarterly basis or annual basis, or a cash disbursement to stock investors, isn't just a foundation of steady revenue; it's a symbol of a business in worthy monetary health. If a business pays a dividend, look at the times past of their payments. Do they have a history of a cumulative dividend or not? If yes, this is a good sign that shows that such a company could be a reliable or trustworthy one.

- ❖ **Things you should never do when selecting a stock**
- ❖ **Don't purchase on price only.** Don't consider a stock that is rock-bottom just because its price has plunged 10%. Always ensure you totally understand the exact reason and how that value is going to recover. When you are sure about this, selecting a stock won't be a difficult task anymore.

- ❖ **Don't depend entirely on forecaster endorsements:** Specialists' reports can suggest and actually provide some awesome information on the well-being of a company. However, you need to be aware of the fact that they actually turn out biased for 'buy' rankings. But because of that predisposition, a sell evaluation, particularly an innovative sell rating, from a forecaster or analyst can be a warning sign. You need to be on the lookout for some of these so-called analysts.

❖ **Don't be staggered by instability.** There is a ninety percent probability that an individual stock is always going to appear more unstable and unpredictable when compared to a diversified mutual fund. You can examine the 52-week highs and slumps for stocks that you're fascinated with to acquire some perception of how extensively amounts can fluctuate in less than a year or in a year.

❖ **Don't fail to remember to trade.** Definitely, you should have a strategy for how you approach purchasing stocks, but it's just as significant to recognize when to trade. Have a set of standards that will convey to you the exact time to sell: If the corporation scratches its dividend; if the price increases or drops to a definite point; if a forecaster reduces the stock, and so on. Devising a strategy for selling will relieve you from the stress of selling out of anxiety over a temporary move in the market. A strategy for selling can also help you earn your profit.

What are the best platforms for choosing stocks?

Here's a list of online platforms where you can select stocks.

* **Ally Invest - Paramount for Inexpensive Trades**

  Paramount for low-cost trades

  Things you should note

  * Little rates and dues and an amazing user border

- ❖ Pros

- ❖ Rock-bottom rates

- ❖ Stress-free admittance point

- ❖ Cons

- ❖ No prospects interchange

Why you should consider it

❖ **Rock-bottom charges**

At $4.95 a piece trade, with virtually no inoperativeness burden and a $50 complete outgoing allocation fee, invests imbursement construction is about as curtailed as you'll realize. Although, a cluster of thoughtless brokers released their directives in 2017 to be viable with Ally Invests $4.95 flat amount. Ally keeps its superiority with a nil account least and alluring mark-down for dynamic investors — fairness trades drop to $3.95 for customers with 30-plus occupations each quarter or a balance of $100,000.

While some mobile platforms like Robin hood boast totally commission-free stocks and ETFs, Ally Invests platform and resources keeps its edge with eminent research and tools, which includes access to its online trader system.

❖ **Easy entry point**

Despite the fact that Ally invest offers attractive pricing, another breath-taking feature it offers is an exemplary platform that affords you unlimited access to the complete world of stocks and ETFs. Where some discount brokers lay emphasis on only one kind of trader (for example, options traders or high-net-worth investors), Ally Invest provides an outstanding knowledge for investors of all kinds. A focus on bargain-basement costs can sometimes be a red flag for excellence, but Ally truly delivers with urbane calculators, profit-loss estimators, and lots more. Ally also offers a healthy exploration library that integrates visual slides and collaborative broadcasting into its market data.

❖ Stellar ratings

It is not an overstatement to say that Ally invest offers one of the most remarkable and impeccable services. Barron's has attested to this fact and given Ally Invests past self, at least four out of five stars for the preceding 10 years, and Ally continues to rack up prestige for its contributions and low commissions from both Barron's and other rating sites like StockBrokers.com.

Points you should cogitate
No prospects trading

❖ If you want to trade "prospects" (contracts to purchase or trade assets in the future), Ally Invest isn't an alternative. That's not rare for an online stock broker — neither Robinhood, Vanguard, nor Fidelity bid prospects trading — but you can do it with some other uppermost preferences, as well as E*TRADE, Charles Schwab, Interactive Brokers, and TD Ameritrade.

❖ **Robinhood - Great for Starters**

If you are just starting out as an investor, Robinhood is a place to be.

❖ Pros

❖ Accessible trading policy

❖ No directive fees

❖ Great beginner-friendly app

❖ Cons

❖ No bonds, mutual funds, futures, or short-selling

Why you should consider it
Comprehensible trading platform

❖ Robinhood is unarguably one of the best online trading platform and a force to reckon with in online business since it was established in the year 2013 by two Stanford alums. Robin-hood revealed their undertaking was inspired by the

Occupy Wall Street demonstrations and indicated in the company's name. The vision is to make investing more reasonably priced and more reachable to millennials. Robin hood's trading interface — both via its mobile app and its website — has turned out to be the most comprehensible of all contenders, which has made it a faultless selection for the first-time dealer. The design is uncluttered, collaborating, and relaxed to pilot. "Robinhood is a worthy fit for innovative investors because it bargains a smooth, modern app that permits you to trade professionally," says a particular stock market analyst and investing and wealth management reporter at Bank rate. "And of course, it's unrestricted with no charge, permitting you to invest money that would have otherwise gone into a broker's pocket."

❖ **No commission fees**

Contrary to the laid down procedures of several online trading platforms, Robinhood doesn't charge a commission fee every time you buy or sell stocks, ETFs, or options. If you're a professional trader or a greenhorn without much money to spare, Robinhood is exactly for you. It is an amazing alternative to the $5 to $7 fees per trade presented by opponents. However, Robinhood does rake in "payment for order flow" by negotiating regulatory fees up to the nearest penny and pinching the difference. "That means if you purchase a stock for $100.00, Robinhood gets an amount of 2.6 cents from the market maker," says co-founder and co-CEO Vlad Tenev, whereas "other brokerages receive returns and charge you a per-trade commission fee."

Points you should cogitate

No bonds, mutual funds, futures, or short-selling

❖ One disadvantage of Robinhood's plainness is that as of 2019, it only affords you the opportunity to trade stocks, ETFs, and selections on the platform — not bonds, mutual funds, or futures, and you can't short-sell. But Robinhood is indeed a place for starters and first-time investors. A starter investor will almost certainly want to stick to the fundamentals. If you're fascinated with the idea of bonds and mutual funds, Ally Invest has the best rates. If you want to attempt futures trading, E*TRADE and Charles Schwab are your best bets.

- ❖ **E*TRADE – Great for Vigorous Traders**

GREAT FOR VIGOROUS TRADERS

Another great accessible platform for energetic traders

- ❖ Pros

- ❖ Volume reductions for recurrent trades

- ❖ Education-heavy platform

- ❖ Low minutest account equilibrium

- ❖ Cons

- ❖ Marginally-advanced commissions

❖ **Why you should consider it**

❖ **Volume deductions for regular trades**

❖ While E*TRADE's starting point fees are a slight high ($6.95 for stocks/ETFs, $6.95 and over 75 cents per deal for selections) associated to Ally Invest, Charles Schwab, and Fidelity, E*TRADE does offer dimensions' markdowns. If you happen to make more than 30 stock/ETFs trades per quarter, the fee lowers to a very competitive $4.95, and if you trade more than 30 selections per quarter, the contract fee reduces to 50 cents. That makes E*TRADE a very attractive fit for dynamic traders who keep a handy eye on the market.

❖ **Education-heavy platform**

❖ Two things an innovative investor needs from their online stock trading platform are an informal learning curve and lots of opportunities to develop. E*TRADE has both. Its platform brags an archive of instructive videos, articles, and webinars for every type of investor. Once you've grasped the basics, read up on market news, reports, and commentary from E*TRADE analysts. You can also take advantage of one-on-one support: Branch appointments are open to book, and online chat tools and round-the-clock hotline are there to monitor and coach you from wherever in the world.

❖ **Low minutest account equilibrium**

❖ E*TRADE does necessitate a stock minimum for first-hand brokerage accounts ($500), which may appear like more than a learner would like to throw in. But that much is needed to experience real development, and compared to the least of traditional brokerages, $500 is an extremely hospitable beginning. Moreover, if you can constrain to a $10,000 deposit, you can get 60 days of commission-free trades.

- ❖ **Points you should cogitate**

- ❖ **Marginally advanced commissions**

- ❖ The only real downside to E*TRADE: Commission fees twitch at $6.95. It's not until investors have made more than 30 trades per quarter that the fees reduce to $4.95, which Ally Invest, Charles Schwab, and Fidelity compromise upfront. But while E*TRADE taxes a sharper charge at this point, there are no additions for cheap stocks or dormancy.

- ❖ **Best Platform Design: TD Ameritrade**

TD Ameritrade is a dominant, exquisitely-designed platform.

- ❖ Pros

- ❖ Supportive platform for learners

- ❖ Influential platform for experts

- ❖ Cons

- ❖ More lavish than mark-down brokerages

❖ **Why you should consider it**

❖ **Supportive platform for learners**

❖ TD Ameritrade propositions two super amazing platforms, specially premeditated for two different kinds of investors. Both platforms are permitted to use by any investor with a TD Ameritrade account. The web-based Trade Designer, though often in the private eye of think or swim, is rationalized and laid-back to use. It will charm beginning investors or anyone who desires an abridged edifying interface. Its tab-based steering lets users flip between trading tools and account synopsis, plus charts, stock screeners, heat maps, and more.

Influential platform for Experts

❖ Think-or-swim, on the other hand, is a driving force premeditated for the advanced. This desktop presentation regularly shelves awards for its grander tools and structures, things any

other broker would bill a superior for —
research reports, simultaneous data, charts,
technical studies. Also included: customizable
workspaces, all-encompassing third-party
examination, a flourishing trader chat room,
and a fully practical mobile app.

❖ Think-or-swim is a specific standout in
selections trading, with options-trading tabs
(just click "spread" if you want a spread and
"single order" if you want one leg), plus links
that elucidate the plans on the command page.
Its Tactic Roller feature allows investors to
generate custom enclosed calls and then roll
those positions from termination to expiration.

❖ **Points you should cogitate**

❖ **More lavish than mark-down brokerages**

❖ TD Ameritrade has been an influential player
in the online stock trading environment for
years. The reverse side to such full-bodied
platforms? Price. Even though TD Ameritrade

dropped its fees in 2017 from $9.99 to $6.95, pretty much every other chief discount broker reduced its prices, too. TD Ameritrade continues to be one of the more luxurious choices out there, even with more than 100 commission-free ETFs. Though its assessing structure is more expensive than those of some of the other discount brokers, there are many traders who think it's a first-class trading platform.

Quality Examination and Tools:

Fidelity

- ❖ Pros

- ❖ Smooth and highly-effective platform

- ❖ First-class research

- ❖ Cons

- ❖ Not all tools are available to all customers

- ❖ **Why you should consider it**

❖ **Smooth and highly effective platform**

❖ Fidelity's platform wins for comprehensible strategy, with apparatuses to help take the presumption out of discovery funds and prying out policies. Fidelity's platform lets you discover your selections with a smooth and spontaneous design, comprehensive with color-coded positions and graphs that call out what's imperative. You can sort stocks by size, enactment, and even standards like sales development or profit growth. Want to sort ETFs by the segments they emphasize on or their expenditures? Finished. There's even a box to see if you desire to discover only Fidelity's commission-free contributions. A few other discount brokers do offer screeners, but none match Fidelity's complexity and usability.

❖ **First-class research**

❖ In terms of adequate research, Fidelity is in a confederation of its own. The knowledgeably curious can plunge into research from more than 20 suppliers, which includes Recognia, Ned Davis, and McLean Capital Administration. Fidelity's Learning Centre featured videos are prearranged by topic, but they don't stop after clarifying the notion; they also cover how to relate doctrines to your own Fidelity investments.

* ❖ **Points you should cogitate**

* ❖ **Not all tools are available to all customers**

* ❖ Awkwardly, some of Fidelity's innovative tools are only accessible to high-volume traders: Charting with Recognia necessitates a noteworthy 120 trades per year to use, and its Vigorous Trader Pro necessitates 36 trades per year.

* ❖ **Additional Online Stock Trading Sites to Consider**

- ❖ **Charles Schwab - Great for Proficient Traders**

- ❖ Like Fidelity and Vanguard, <u>Charles Schwab</u> is one of the older brick-and-mortar investment brokers that effectively rationalized its exchange platform for the Internet Age. Charles Schwab still happens to be the best choice for advanced traders who want a full battery of selections (stocks, ETFs, options, bonds, mutual funds, futures) and an extraordinary suite of exploration tools. Best of all, even with all the benefits Charles Schwab offers, it's still one of the lowest-cost trading platforms, with low-priced fees than E*TRADE or TD Ameritrade on most trades.

- ❖ **Vanguard - Pre-eminent for Retirement Investors**

- ❖ Since <u>Vanguard</u> is the principal mutual fund bill payer in the world, it doesn't require a fee for the majority of mutual fund trades.

Nevertheless, there are several other kinds of trading which are more luxurious, with $7 per selection and up to $20 per stock/ETF. For that motive, Vanguard isn't a recommended platform for starters or low-volume dealers. Nevertheless, Vanguard is an outstanding option for retirement investors involved in long-term, high-volume incomes, or those considering a place to take their IRA. In fact, Vanguard is one great selection for the finest IRA accounts.

- ❖ **Interactive Brokers – Cheapest and affordable Commission Rates**

- ❖ When it comes to volume, <u>Interactive Brokers</u> is strictly the prevalent online stock trading platform in the U.S. It also publicizes itself as the "lowest cost broker," and for respectable reason: It only charges a disturbingly low $0.005 per trade on stocks, ETFs, options, bonds, mutual funds, and futures (plus a 7 cent per contract fee for options). Theoretically, that's still complex than Robinhood, but Robinhood only deals in stocks, ETFs, and options. Just as mentioned earlier, Robinhood does scan some money off the top of trades via "fee for order flow").

❖ If you're an energetic, high-volume dealer and you want to try your hand in all kinds of assets, Interactive Brokers is a wonderful option, since you can trade just about anything without losing $5 to $7 on every deal. The platform interface isn't nearly as comprehensible as Robinhood's, nor as spontaneous as TD Ameritrade's; nevertheless, if you're the kind of depositor who'd benefit the most from Collaborating Brokers (i.e., an experienced one), you'll know your way around a candlestick diagram definitely.

Chapter 5

MARKET MASTERY

In this chapter, you will get to know exactly how the stock market works and how to efficiently analyze the stock market.

Now that you are already familiar with some of the platforms for buying stocks, the next question on your mind might be how to analyze a stock. Do you happen to be a victim of analysis paralysis? Do you have a stock you are interested in purchasing but you don't have the vaguest idea of where to even begin a suitable analysis? This chapter will answer every question. Sit back and enjoy every detail provided.

Investing in this era is a lot more different from how it was done back in the days, 50, or even 20 years, ago. Back then, you could only get some degree of amount of stock data in the day-to-day newspaper. Now it's quite different as there is a wide range of access to an apparently limitless amount of data on every openly traded stock. Of course, this has its own advantages and downsides as well.

One downside is the fact that there's so much information floating around the web which has made a lot of people get lost in the specifics, only those who know exactly where to look can make more conversant investing choices.

You can essentially conduct a detailed examination of any stock in 12 easy steps: a process known as the Nasdaq Dozen.

Just to put this out there, it is imperative to keep in mind that the Nasdaq Dozen is neither a crystal ball nor a warranty of accomplishment. Reasonably, it is a balanced, repeatable process for investigating the most significant essential and practical aspects of any stock.

It is also essential to keep in mind that no stock is 100 percent perfect. If you look clearly enough, you can continually find a problem with a stock. On the other hand, if you look hard enough, you can always find something worthy about a stock. The point is to put your money in stocks that have better prospects.

For an innovative investor, the stock market can appear to be a lot like legitimate gambling. "Females and gents, place your gambles! Unsystematically select a stock based on gut disposition and water cooler conversation! If the price of your stock increases -- and who knows the exact reason? -- you emerge the winner! If it reduces, you lose it all!" Doesn't it seem like the reason a whole lot of people got rich during the dot-com boom -- and why so many others lost their shirts (and of course their life savings) in the recent slump?

This is not the case. But it's so unfortunate that quite a number of innovative and beginning investors actually feel this way about the stock market - as a temporary investment vehicle that either carries huge financial increases or overwhelming losses. With that assertiveness, the stock market is as dependable a form of investment as a game of roulette. However, if you devote more time to learn about stocks and the more you comprehend the true landscape of stock market investment, the healthier and keener you'll be able to manage your income.

The stock market can be frightening, but a little knowledge of how it works can help ease your terrors. Let's begin with some simple definitions. A **share** of stock is factually a part in the possession of a firm. Purchasing a share gives you an entitlement to a part of the properties and pays of that firm. **Possessions** comprise the whole thing the business possesses (buildings, equipment, trademarks), and **earnings** are all of the money the corporation brings in from trading its merchandises and services.

Why exactly do you think a company would want to allocate or distribute its assets and earnings with the over-all public? Because it's in dire need of money, of course. Corporations only have two ways to make money to cover start-up costs or enlarge the trade: It can either lend money from (a procedure called **debt financing**) or trade stock (also known as **equity financing**).

The drawback of borrowing money is that the business has to refund the loan with a particular amount of interest. By trading stock, on the other hand, the company makes money with almost no strings attached. There is no interest to pay and no obligation to even refund money back at all. Even better, equity financing allocates the risk of doing business amongst a large pool of stockholders. If the business fails, the originators don't lose all of their money; several portion of other individuals' hard-earned money is lost instead.

Possibly the finest way to clarify how stocks and the stock market actually work is to use an illustration. We'll use a theoretical food business to help elucidate the rudimentary principles behind giving out and purchasing stock.

Let's assume that you've always dreamed of opening a cafeteria. You love food so much, and you've done your study to figure out how expensive it is to open a cafeteria, including how much money you could anticipate to make each year in profit. The construction and apparatus would cost $500,000 up front, and annual expenditures (ingredients, employee salaries, utilities) would charge an extra $250,000. With yearly earnings of $325,000, you expect to earn a $75,000 profit every year. Sounds interesting!

The only issue is that you don't have $750,000 (building + equipment + expenses) in cash to cover all of those costs. You could go out to borrow this amount of money, but that accumulates interest. What about looking for investors who would give you money in exchange for a part of the proprietorship of the cafeteria?

This is the rationality that businesses use when they decide to issue stock to private or unrestricted stockholders. They rely on the fact that the business will be lucrative enough that investors will see a good profit. In this instance, if stockholders paid an aggregate of $750,000 for shares in your restaurant, they could expect to make $75,000 per annum. That's a concrete 10 percent profit.

Being the proprietor of the cafeteria, you can fix the original value of the business, as well as the entire number of shares of stock you want to issue to the general public. Fascinatingly, the value of the food business doesn't have to draw parallels with the definite value of the assets or the business's existing productivity. You can fix the amount so that it replicates the forthcoming value of the venture. For instance, if you fix the price at $750,000, investors could assume a 10 percent return. If you fix the price at twice that much, $1,500,000, investors would still get a reputable 5 percent return.

If you dispute a lot of shares, that would bring down the price of each individual share, possibly making the stock more eye-catching to solitary investors. Another deliberation is possession. Each individual who purchases a share of stock fundamentally owns a piece of the company and has a say in how the business is run. We'll discuss more about stockholders. However, the focus now is for you to comprehend that, as the proprietor, you may request to purchase a mainstream of the obtainable shares yourself so that you continue to be in majority control of the business. Now, we will be discussing how to analyze the stock market.

How to analyze the stock market?

Investors rely on stock analysis to find hypothetically lucrative stocks. Common ways to examine stock include technical and fundamental analysis. Several constituents fall under fundamental analysis, which includes investigation of a business's price-to-earnings ratio, earnings per share, book value, and return on even-handedness. Many stockholders also use the endorsements of financial predictors to evaluate a stock. The type of stock analysis you implement is based on individual inclination. Recognize the diverse ways to analyze a stock to find the technique that best turns your monetary goals.

Technical analysis

The technical analysis essentially looks into the supply and demand of a stock contained by the market. Stockholders who make use of technical analysis believe that a stock's chronological presentation specifies how the stock will perform in the imminent. Little attention is given to the worth of the corporation. The technical analysis places substantial emphasis on the learning of trends, charts, and designs.

P/e ratio

One of the commonest methods of analyzing a stock is studying its price-to-earnings ratio. You compute the P/E ratio by allotting the stock's market value per share by its earnings per share. To find out the value of a stock, investors compare a stock's P/E ratio to those of its contenders and business standards. Lower P/E ratios are seen as approving by investors.

Earnings per share

A company's earnings per share display how professionally its revenue is smooth down to investors. An accumulative EPS is taken as a decent sign by depositors. According to NASDAQ, the advanced a company's EPS, the further the value of your shares, because investors seek to obtain a business's stock when payouts are great.

Peg ratio

The price-to-earnings development ratio takes the P/E ratio a step forward by considering the development of a business. To calculate the PEG, you divide the P/E ratio by the 12-month growth rate. You estimate the future growth rate by looking at the company's historical development rate. Investors characteristically consider a stock valuable if the PEG is lower than 1.

Book value

Another technique used to analyze a stock is shaping a firm's price-to-book ratio. Investors characteristically use this technique to discover highly developed companies that are underrated. The procedure for the P/B ratio equals the market price of a corporation's stock divided by its book value of equity. Book value of equity is gotten by misusing the book value of obligations from the book value of possessions.

Stockholders consider a low P/B ratio as a red flag that the stock is hypothetically belittled.

Return on Equity

Stockholders use return on equity to regulate how well a corporation yields positive revenues for its stockholders. Analyzing ROE can help you discover businesses that are profit producers. ROE is computed by dividing net income by average shareholders' equity. A continual increase in ROE is a good sign to investors.

Analyst recommendations

Many investors use analyst endorsements to rapidly examine a stock. Analysts perform a wide-ranging ultimate and practical investigation, and they issue purchase or vend endorsements. Before concluding to purchase or vend shares, investors characteristically use analyst authorizations in combination with a stock analysis method.

What is a Bull Market?

A bull market can be defined as the circumstance of a money market, of a cluster of securities, in which there is an inflation in the value of the market or there is an anticipated increase in the market value. The word bull market is basically used in reference to the stock market but can also be used to refer to anything which is traded. These include bonds, real estate, currencies, and merchandises. Because there is always an increase and fall in the prices of securities unceasingly during trading, the term "bull market" is typically set aside for lengthy periods in which a great portion of security prices are rising. Bull markets tend to last for months or even years.

Comprehending Bull markets

The bull market is actually branded by buoyancy, investor assurance, and prospects that strong results should last for a protracted period of time. It is problematic to forecast reliably when the inclinations in the market might transform. Part of the struggle is that emotional effects and assumption may occasionally play a great role in the market place.

There isn't an exact and worldwide metric used to recognize a bull market. However, conceivably the most common explanation of a bull market is a condition in which stock prices rise by 20%, typically after a descent of 20% and before a subsequent 20% degeneration. Since bull markets are tough to forecast, analysts can characteristically only distinguish this sensation after it has happened. A distinguished bull market in topical history was the era between 2003 and 2007. Throughout this time, the S&P 500 amplified by a momentous margin after a preceding decline; as the 2008 monetary crisis took effect, most important deteriorations happened again after the bull market run.

Features of a Bull Market

Bull markets usually take place when the economy is firming up or when it is already robust. They tend to occur in line with the sturdy gross domestic product (GDP) and a reduction in joblessness and will often overlap with a rise in business profits. <u>Investor assurance</u> will also incline to ascent throughout a bull market period. The general demand for stocks will be optimistic, along with the inclusive quality of the market. In accumulation, there will be a broad-spectrum upsurge in the amount of IPO activity throughout bull markets.

Remarkably, some of the dynamics stated above are more effortlessly computable than others. While business incomes and joblessness are measurable, it can be more challenging to measure the over-all tone of market clarification, for illustration. Supply and demand for securities will fluctuate: supply will be feeble while request will be sturdy. Investors will be keen on procuring securities, while few will be eager to trade. In a bull market, investors are more keen to take part in the (stock) market in order to make profits.

Bull vs. Bear Markets

The bear market is the direct opposite of a bull market; the bear market is described by dwindling prices and characteristically masked in cynicism. The usually held belief about the origin of these terms proposes that the use of "bull" and "bear" to label markets comes from the way the wildlife in question attack their adversaries. A bull shoves its horns up into the air, while a bear jabs its paws plunging. These movements are descriptions for the movement of a market. If the inclination of the market is up, it's a bull market. If the trend is down, it is known as a bear market.

Bull and bear markets frequently correspond with the financial cycle, which comprises of four phases: increase, peak, contraction, and trench. The beginning of a bull market is often a principal pointer of financial development. Because public emotion about future economic circumstances pushes stock prices, the market regularly increases even before broader financial measures, such as gross domestic product (GDP) growth, begin to pick up. Similarly, bear markets typically set in before financial reduction takes hold. A look back at a characteristic U.S. slump discloses a dwindling stock market several months ahead of GDP weakening.

How to use the bull market to your advantage?

Stockholders who desire to benefit from a bull market should purchase on time so as to use this period to their advantage. This is a time to purchase stocks at rising prices and trade them when they've touched their crest. Although it is difficult to regulate or know exactly when the extremity and ultimate will occur, most damages will be marginal and are typically impermanent. Below, we'll discover numerous conspicuous policies investors apply during bull market eras. Nevertheless, because it is challenging to evaluate the state of the market as it exists presently, these plans involve at least some degree of peril altogether.

❖ **Purchase and keep**

One of the most rudimentary policies in investing is the process of purchasing a specific security and keeping it, hypothetically to trade it at an advanced date. This approach essentially involves self-reliance on the part of the stockholder: why should you keep a security unless you anticipate its value to rise? For this motive, the buoyancy that comes along with bull markets aids to fuel the technique of purchase and keep.

❖ Augmented Buy and Hold

Augmented buy and hold is a disparity on the up-front buy and hold tactic, and it involves extra risk. The evidence behind the augmented buy and hold tactic is that an investor will endure to add to his or her holdings in a specific security so long as it endures to upsurge in worth. One common method for cumulative holdings suggests that a stockholder will buy a supplementary fixed amount of shares for every escalation in the stock price of a pre-set quantity.

❖ Retracement Additions

This can be defined as a short time where there is a reverse in the entire inclination of a security's worth. Even during a bull market, it's improbable that stock values will only rise. Moderately, it is possible there is a turnout of shorter eras of time in which small dints occur as well, even as the over-all inclination lasts upward. Some stockholders watch for retracements within a bull market and move to purchase in the course of these periods. The philosophy behind this approach is that, presuming that the bull market lingers, the value of the security in question will swiftly move back up, retroactively supplying the investor with a bargain-basement acquisition price.

❖ **Full Fluctuate Trading**

Conceivably the most belligerent way of endeavoring to take advantage of a bull market is the process known as <u>full swing or fluctuate trading</u>. Investors exploiting this approach will take very vigorous roles: They have to be actively involved in using short-selling and other procedures to try to crush out concentrated gains as changes occur within the framework of a grander bull market. It is important to note that:

- ❖ A bull market is an era marked by the continuous rise in the prices of assets or security.

- ❖ The regularly accepted explanation of a bull market is when stock prices rise by 20% after two regressions of 20% each.

- ❖ Traders hire a diversity of tactics, such as augmented buy and hold and retracement, to make money off bull markets.

A typical example of a bull market.

The most productive bull market in contemporary American history commenced at the end of the recession period in 1982 and resolved during the dotcom bust in 2000. In the course of this profane bull market — a term that symbolizes a bull market enduring many years — the Dow Jones Industrial Average (DJIA) averaged 16.8% yearly revenues. The NASDAQ, a tech-heavy altercation, amplified its worth five-fold between 1995 and 2000, mounting from 1,000 to over 5,000. A long-drawn-out bear market shadowed the 1982-2000 bull market. From 2000 to 2009, the market wriggled to inaugurate equilibrium and supplied mediocre yearly returns of - 6.2%. Nevertheless, 2009 saw the twitch of ten-year bull market track. Forecasters believe that the previous bull market started on March 9, 2009, and was principally led by an increase in technology stocks.

How to get ready for the stock market

Stock market bangs or crashes are typically a result of more than one factor. In fact, there are often two sets of causes of a crash. One set of circumstances generates the environment for the sell-off, and additional set of elements prompt the commencement of the sell-off. Just because there is a market fizz, it doesn't mean a crash will occur. Ordinarily, something needs to happen to cause stockholders to commence selling and customers to step away from the typical market.

Extraordinary estimates, dwindling or unsatisfactory business earnings, bankruptcies, dwindling customer expenditure, rising increase, a downturn or motionless economic development, and geopolitical proceedings can all create the environment for an alteration, a crash or a bear market. The commencement of a sell-off is customarily activated by dwindling liquidity.

Falling liquidity may happen if banks stop spreading credit or if a controller intensifies the margin necessities for dealers. Occasionally when a central bank increases interest rates, banks will instigate to call in some of their advances, activating a shortage of liquidity in the market. The humblest clarification is that at some point the money runs out. Markets rise while stockholders continue to purchase, and when they begin to go into debt, markets plummet. The rigorous cause of a crash is often tranquil to recognize in retrospection but difficult to see at the time. So, when will there be a crash in the stock market again? There is no specific answer to this question. The FAANG stocks (Facebook, Apple, Amazon, Netflix, and Google) have commanded the bull market over the preceding 9 years. If these stocks fail to hold onto their income momentum going, investors may lose assurance in the market. So far, only

Facebook and Netflix have dissatisfied stockholders, while Apple continues to be a force to reckon with.

The CAPE ratio (which is the same as Shiller P/E ratio) is a long period intermittently attuned amount of equity assessments formulated by the appreciated economist Robert Shiller. The CAPE ratio has been at an archaeologically high position for numerous years, although high estimates alone do not mean a crash is looming. Whether US stock prices today are in a stock fizz or not is arguable. In broad-spectrum, fizzes do not unavoidably imply a crash, except there is a catalyst.

An intensification of the trade war with China and Europe could sooner or later lead to earnings impetus dwindling. Unmaintainable levels of dues in China and other developing markets could also activate a crash. If China's stock market were to crash, that alone possibly would not initiate a bear market around the world.

Nevertheless, if China's economy wavers, it might. Geopolitical uproar concerning North Korea, Iran, Syria, or Russia could also become a facilitator if things worsen enough. It's most likely that the next market crash, whenever it happens, will be the consequence of a perfect blizzard caused by numerous factors. But, since it's not something that can be easily predicted, it's best to deliberate on being equipped for a crash whenever it may take place.

One needs to be very equipped and ready for a stock market crash. For green-horns and beginner investors, it's worth memorizing the following:

- ❖ In the long run, investors are remunerated for taking on risk. Running away from risks completely means sidestepping returns. Several specialists have foretold a 50% crash every year since 2009. If you had shadowed their counsel, you might have been among the people who lost out on more than 200% of profits just because they were scared of investing as a result of an impending crash which never occurred.

- ❖ The world's most prominent investors have succeeded in making returns over the long run in spite of several market crashes. They have years that worked out well and of course the opposite. However, they have had more favorable years than less favorable ones.

❖ There is no solitary resolution that will keep your assets from every bear market. Every crash is altered, and sometimes safe-havens don't turn out to be as harmless as they were hypothetical to be.

❖ Unavoidably some of the venture choices you make might not end up being the best. This is why every investor is advised to expand their portfolio and not put their eggs in one basket.

In other words, bear markets are part of capitalizing. You can't run away from them altogether. However, you can always ensure you do not get wiped out by a bear market. The Golden Rule is to **diversify**, and occasionally **rebalance** your assortment. When a modification, stock market crash or bear market originates the stocks that drop the most are those that are dealing at the highest evaluations, those with the most dues, and those with the lowest restrictions.

These stocks are referred to as high beta stocks, as they outdo on the way up and drift on the way down. Throughout a bull market, these high beta stocks are frequently the stocks that perform the best. As an outcome, they will mature into the leading positions in your assortment. That's why it's a noble thing to rebalance your assortment and make sure the premium of these *"high beta"* stocks aren't too high. Here are some more ways to organize for a stock market crash:

- ❖ Shift to self-justifying asset classes and safe haven investments

- ❖ Use stop loss guidelines to make balanced decisions

- ❖ Grasp enough cash to take advantage of a stock market crash

Shift to self-justifying asset classes and safe haven investments

To diminish damages during a bear market, you can spread part of your portfolio across the subsequent stock market sectors and other asset classes that are considered defensive:

- ❖ Defensive stocks

- ❖ High-quality dividend stocks and blue-chip stocks

- ❖ Precious metals

- ❖ Bonds

- ❖ Hedge funds

- ❖ Cryptocurrencies

Defensive stocks

Non-cyclical consumer stocks and conveniences trade at lower assessments and typically continue to make proceeds during slumps. These are the businesses that trade goods and services that are disbursed regardless of the economic cycle – narcotics, cleaning products, groceries, and gas are good instances.

High-quality dividend stocks and blue-chip stocks

Concrete yet boring establishments are often ignored and unnoticed in the course of bull markets when stockholders focus on development stocks. When stocks instigate to slither, a flight to eminence will often ensue, causing these stocks to leave behind. It really boils down to keeping the stocks that will endure a downturn.

Precious metals

Several precious metals like silver and gold are extensively well-thought-out as safe-haven assets and have archeologically outdone in the course of most (but not all) market crashes. You can purchase precious metal ETFs, bodily metal, or you can purchase shares in valuable metal manufacturers and excavating companies.

Bonds

Factually, bonds have outdone stocks throughout virtually every stock market crash and bear market.

Nevertheless, with bond yields at ancient slumps, they do convey more risk now than they did years back. They are worth contemplation; just be cautious of having too much contact to bonds.

Hedge funds

Hedge funds are a substitute for investors with huge and enormous assortments. Hedge funds use an amalgamation of long and short situations, and other policies to produce returns irrespective of the direction of the general market. However, when bearing in mind hedge funds, you should step with restraint and do a thorough investigation. Some hedge funds have done very great, specifically during bear markets – but numerous others have done very poorly. The fact that it is referred to as a hedge fund doesn't guarantee its good performance during a market crash.

Cryptocurrencies

Though recognition of cryptocurrencies as an investment has been made, a lot of people still consider it a very risky investment. Bitcoins are sometimes considered as a safe-haven just in case of a universal crash due to its regionalized nature, the low connection with the stock markets and the restricted supply. There is no dependable data obtainable on how cryptocurrencies act throughout a stock market crash. Nevertheless, if you're enthusiastic to take the risk, tallying a small fraction of Bitcoin or cryptocurrency stocks to an expanded portfolio could be a meaningful investment choice.

Use stop-loss guidelines to make sensible decisions

If you are worried about how much you could miss on some of your principal positions, you can also consider using stop-loss orders to alleviate potential losses. For each stock, you can fix a few price levels below practical maintenance where you will commence to moderate the extent of the situation. It's advised to ensure this is done long before stock prices begin to plummet so that your choices are balanced and not sentimental. Stop-loss is not normally a tactic used by long-term stockholders. Nevertheless, they can help you cope with the psychological effect that comes with the bear market.

Hold enough cash to benefit from a stock market crash

Feasibly the most appropriate way to hedge your portfolio against a crash is to make sure you always have a vigorous portion of it allocated to cash. The amount you allot to cash is really determined by how much unpredictability you are happy to cope with. More cash means you only lose little. However, you will most likely lose out on revenues in the long run. A lower cash equilibrium will undoubtedly lead to advanced general returns but will also mean sophisticated instability.

One other benefit of holding cash, particularly after an extended bull market, is that you will be able to purchase low-priced stock when a crash does happen. Always keep in mind. after a crash, the peril is much inferior – that's when you want to assign more to stocks, and not as much of two defensive assets, precious metals, bonds and cash.

Conclusion: Formulate a plan for the next stock market crash

As you have been made to understand, preparing for a stock market crash goes far beyond forecast. *"Specialists"* forecast crashes all the time, and most of the time, they might not be right. If you pay attention to all these crash forecasts, you will end up bringing up the rear out on the upside. And nevertheless, you should never be in a situation where your portfolio gets wiped out as a result of the crash. Getting yourself ready for a crash means you ought to diversify your portfolio. You can mitigate the effects of a crash by assigning to defensive and blue-chip stocks, bonds, gold, and cash. Having some currencies in your assortment also lets you buy back into the market at minor levels. The existing stock market is equitably luxurious, but there are no emblems of an impending crash. However, that doesn't mean market circumstances can't alter quickly. That's why you should always be prepared for the "coming" or impending crash.

Chapter 6

DIVERSIFICATION & AVOIDING THE PITFALLS

Since you are the one who is in charge of managing your own portfolio, there is a great need to understand and comprehend how essential diversification is to you as an investor. Although no one prays to encounter a loss, you need to brace up yourself for "not-so-good days". When that happens and you run into a loss, you need other reserves to counterweight the degeneration. Diversification guarantees that by not "putting all your eggs in one basket," you will not be setting yourself up for an unnecessary heartbreak when something goes wrong. Trusting all your finances in the hands of one company might not be too good an idea.

Confused on how to commence?

Many investors diversify by purchasing diverse types of funds. Advisors recommend opening with a broad-based index fund that simply tries to reflect the presentation of the S&P 500. Then you could supplement that index fund with a fund that acquisitions share in foreign corporations; one that comprises of shares of small growth businesses; one that capitalizes in bonds and an additional one that purchases shares in real estate investment trusts (REITs).

There are several websites such as Morningstar where you can discover investigation and information about mutual funds to get you on track. Brokerages will characteristically bargain what is called a "prospectus" of a stock market, and it is important to go through these before creating investment decisions. By expanding your assortment, you'll give yourself a chance to develop your money regardless of the ups and downs that come with capitalizing.

Asset Allocation

Over the years, one of the most common form of diversification is asset allocation. By having rudiments of various investment classes in your assortment—which includes stocks, bonds, cash, real estate, gold, or other merchandises—you can safeguard your portfolio from losing the value that it might if it only controlled one failing asset classification.

When stock prices plummet, for example, bond prices often increase because investors move their money into what is well-thought-out a less perilous venture. So an assortment that comprised shares and bonds would perform differently from one that comprised just shares at the period of a crash. It is also intelligent to expand in the interior of asset sessions. Stockholders who put their money on technology shares in the year 2000 came back crying after there was a market crash and technology stocks hurriedly performed contrarily to their expectations. In like manner, shares remained beaten down in late 2007 and early 2008 as a result of the subprime mortgage crisis.

Also, if it appears unwise to invest all your money in only one segment, this would be exactly the same with a particular stock. That's what many stockholders did in the late 1990s, often as workers of tech corporations who permitted their holdings to become unbalanced in their employer's stock. These fundamentally one-stock assortments were parallel to flagpole sitters in the 1930s, suspended high in the air with only a stretched, narrow pole for sustenance.

Subsequently, in the month of September, they had fallen to underneath six dollars. It didn't mount back until the 12th month in the year 2007.

So the two steps to diversification are to spread your money among various asset categories, then further assign those funds *surrounded by* each category. A smart tactic for individual investors is to diversify via mutual funds. Because mutual funds are groups of stocks, you'll be expanded to a confident degree by definition.

Below are four steps to help you get ready for income diversification.

Step 1: Make sure your assortment has many diverse investments

ETFs & mutual funds

An uncomplicated way to do this is by acquiring ETFs, index funds, or mutual funds. ETFs and mutual funds act as a carrier of different stocks— providing you with instant diversification. They trade inversely, so you'll want to read about each in detail before purchasing them, but they're an outstanding method to expand without getting overly complex.

Index funds

One other great option is the use of index funds; this is because they consist of stocks that reflect a precise index—such as the S&P 500. Your variation may be a little more restricted here, but it's still a sound selection to contemplate.

A suitably-diversified investment portfolio should contain the following:

❖ Money

❖ Shares

❖ Bonds

- ❖ Exchange-traded funds

- ❖ Mutual funds

Step 2: Diversify within separate kinds of investments

Select investments with various rates of returns

This turns out more thought-provoking when you're purchasing individual stocks since you'll want to put in a reasonable amount of money to make the cost of exchange worth it. For instance, you don't want a situation where you have to spend $10 to purchase one share of stock for $200. You should put in a larger chunk, so you save money on fees. As a result of this, several people keep a handful of stocks in their portfolio, which opens them to a lot of risk.

So when investing in stocks, for example, don't quintessence on a single stock or a few stocks but reasonably, diverse stocks in VARIOUS sectors. It's also indispensable to have stocks with mixed-income, development, market capitalization among other metrics. When putting your money in things like bonds, select bonds with different credit qualities, duration, and maturities.

Make Use of Ally Invest

If you're looking to hedge into the stock market, contemplate Ally Invest. This has been mentioned in the previous chapter.

Step 3: You should weigh investments with fluctuating risk

Select investments with numerous rates of profit

In order to diversify your portfolio in the most proper manner, select various investments whose rate of return is different to safeguard considerable improvements for positive investments counterbalance losses in other investments.

Keep in mind, although the purpose is to diminish risk, you aren't constrained to blue-chip stocks only.

Overseas or External stocks

A good procedure to practice here is to look at overseas stocks. Imported stocks from other countries tend to perform a little inversely and characteristically poise out a domestic-heavy investment assortment nicely. You can also look at small-cap or mid-cap stocks, which are undeveloped, and more unpredictable stocks.

Step 4: Reshuffle your assortment frequently

Make Use of Bloom

Unlike the view of so many people, diversification isn't something you do once and abandon. You should reexamine your assortment often and make alterations consequently when the risk level isn't reliable with your monetary goals or approach. I endorse reshuffling your assortment at least twice every year. Or, you could use a provision like Bloom, which is a 401(k) optimization tool which ensures the durability of your 401k.

Employ the service of a robo-advisor

In accumulation, if you find it stressful to keep purchasing stocks and trading them to smoothen out your assortment, you will do well with the service of a robo-advisor such as Betterment, which will mechanically rebalance your collection for you and keep you optimally expanded.

A diversified portfolio should include:

Domestic stocks

Purchasing stocks affords you a prospect to <u>own a fraction of a firm</u> which comes with welfares such as dividend payouts and wealth expansions when the stock upsurges in price over time. Domestic stocks should be a momentous fragment of your investment assortment as long as they bargain great prospects for development in the long-standing.

The world's utmost investor, Warren Buffet demonstrates in detail how to diversify when capitalizing in domestic stocks with his top five stock picks being Apple, Wells Fargo, Kraft Heinz Company, BOA (Bank of America) and Coca-Cola. The stocks signify different corporations in diverse sectors.

Bonds

Bonds actually bid unvarying interest income. They are a smaller amount of unpredictable stocks which makes them a worthy "pillow" during impulsive activities in the stock markets.

Stocks should be a noteworthy quota of a portfolio for an investor absorbed in more on the protection of their investment than development. It is worth observing that bonds don't bid higher yields than stocks in the long term, in maximum cases. Conversely, there are convinced international bonds which provide higher yields.

If you're thinking of going into bonds, you could try this super amazing company called Worthy that's proposing a static 5% yearly interest rate – and respectively, a bond costs just $10. The performance of this company has been really impressive.

Temporary investments

One thing you should not forget to include in your assortment is a list of short-term or temporary certificates of payments as well as money market funds which is very stable and gives you direct access to a list of investments. There are guaranteed insurance Investments such as certificates of deposits are insured/guaranteed by the FDIC making them safer; however, they aren't as liquid as money market funds.

Global stocks

A good mix of universal stocks is endorsed to safeguard your collection against the local stock market "shocks." Stocks allotted by US companies act differently from those issued by non-US businesses since they are exposed to various opportunities from several parts of the world.

Sector funds

Just like the name implies, sector funds can be defined as a type of investment fund which has its focus on explicit sectors/fragments of the economy. Possessing this type of fund and including it in your assortment affords you several genuine investment chances in a lot of economic cycles.

Real estate fund

Owning a real estate fund as a part of your assortment, including real estate investment trusts protects you from hyperinflation. You could also take advantage of the very distinctive opportunities that may not be available elsewhere.

Commodity-focused funds

You can get your portfolio protected against inflation by investing in Equity funds which focus on commodities such as gas, minerals, oil, etc. Investors are also saved from the perils that are connected with commodities since investing in commodities is advised for experienced investors only.

Asset allocation funds

People who are keen and enthusiastic about investing but do not have enough professional ideas and time to develop their own diversified portfolio.

Reasons for income diversification

Diversifying decreases the insecurity of investing

Every financial market comes with a certain degree of uncertainty or insecurity. Investing all you have in stocks can actually mean you stand the risk of losing everything if there is a stock market crash. This is the same as every other investment like the real estate market, commodities markets, currencies, and any other investment. Nevertheless, you need to understand that it is almost impossible for a crash to occur in all the markets at the same time in the same way.

This is the case with assets class investment as well. For example, two stocks of various companies in various sectors experience fluctuations in different manners. When you diversify your income by investing in different investments through different sectors, the prospect of losing a substantial amount of money or your total investment is very low.

Warren Buffet once noted that diversification of your income is "protection against ignorance" making it redundant when you know exactly what you are doing. Nevertheless, Buffet is already a veteran wealthy investor. He has devoted several years and has also become proficient at the game of investing and has equipped himself with several experiences which are far beyond the reach of commonplace investors.

Chapter 7

REINVESTING

What do you understand by a dividend reinvestment plan?

A dividend reinvestment plan (DRIP) can be defined as a program, which gives investors an opportunity to plow their cash dividends into supplementary shares or segmental shares, of the fundamental stock on the dividend payment date. Though this term is often used in reference to any kind of programmed reinvestment procedure organized by brokerage or investment company, it commonly refers to a recognized program presented by a visibly traded company to prevailing stockholders. Close to six hundred and fifty firms and five-hundred closed-end funds presently do so.

Comprehending a Dividend Reinvestment Plan—DRIP

The usual mode of paying dividends to shareholders is either via a check or the depositing of fund into the shareholders' accounts. DRIPs, which are also known as dividend reinvestment programs, allow a shareholder to reinvest the total of a confirmed dividend into supplementary shares, which are purchased straight from the firm. Because shares acquired via a DRIP stereotypically come from the firm's own standby or reserve, they are not expected to be marketable through stock interactions. Shares must be exchanged directly via the company, as well.

Most DRIPs permit investors to acquire shares free of commission or for a minimal fee, and at a momentous reduction to the existing share value. The dollar may be set at a minimum rate. Nevertheless, most do not sanction reinvestments much lesser than $10. Despite the fact that DRIPs are frequently proposed for obtainable shareholders, some companies do make them accessible to new investors, regularly postulating a least possible procurement amount.

While the reinvested dividends are not essentially gotten by the shareholder, they are always reported as payable income (unless they are kept in a tax-privileged account, like an IRA).

How does an investor benefit from drips?

DRIPs give stockholders a means to accrue more shares without necessarily going through the pain of having to pay a certain amount of commission. Although quite a lot of firms actually give shares at a discounted rate via their DRIP from 1% to 10% off the current share price. Between commission free and a discounted rate, the cost foundation for possessing the shares can be considerably subordinate than if the shares were acquired on the public or open market. Fractional shares can also be purchased by investors through DRIPs, therefore, this puts every cent of your money to work. Longstanding, the greatest benefit is the outcome of spontaneous reinvestment on the compounding of revenues. An increase in the price of dividends gives shareholders an opportunity to receive a cumulative amount on every share they possess, which can also obtain a loftier number of shares. Over time, this grows the entire return probability of the investment. Because more shares can be acquired at any time the stock price falls, the enduring possibility for better expansions is amplified.

Benefits of DRIPS to a firm

Companies known for paying dividends actually benefit from DRIPs in several ways. Originally, purchasing a share from a firm in the form of a drip provides the business with more capital.

Furthermore, there is a 10 percent probability of stockholders who are active participants in a drip choosing to trade out their shares when there is a decline in the stock market. This is probably because participants have a tendency to be enduring investors who are aware of the role their dividends play in the abiding development of their assortment. One other influence is that DRIP-purchased shares are not as liquefied as shares obtained on the open market—they can only be exchanged via the establishment.

Reinvesting your dividends basically has to do with acquiring extra shares of stock with the money you get.

On a lot of trading platforms, it is your choice if you want to do this automatically without being directly involved by merely checking a box. Advocates of this tactic highpoint the statistic that the act of acquiring new shares of a stock that you are aware is a dividend-paying one allows you to grow your investment faster than pocketing your dividends and depending on capital income for wealth generation.

Sometimes, certain programs are provided by firms for programmed dividend reinvestment that allows you to obtain supplementary shares at a discounted rate. One very important advantage of dividend reinvestment lies in its capability to develop your wealth silently, so that when you need to diversify your income, especially post-retirement, you already have a steady stream of investment revenue aside.

I believe you are aware of the fact that dividends are essential because the investor is provided with extra money for the settlement of bills, money to shop your groceries and generally increase your standard of living. You can use the dividends to pay your travel bills, medical bills, or simply have it donated to charity. There's so much you could do with the money. The good news, however, is the fact that leaving this substantial amount of money to accrue for some time, can earn you a whopping amount of money if you choose to reinvest it: that is, use them to purchase even *additional* shares of stock that pay dividends in turn. There are stereotypically two means of reinvesting your dividends, one of which is tilling them back into the firm that paid them (this approach can reduce the risk of liquidation for any one firm but announces more social verdict and give way for blunder in the process); the second means is assembling them together and modifying as if they were new cash just like any other payment. Making a decision to reinvest dividends in a positive industry can actually earn you a better compounding rate and wealth formation.

Reinvesting your dividends can actually make a great difference when observing a single company in separation.

How does compound interest work?

If you are bent on managing your finances, one of the most essential concepts you need to get familiar with is the concept of "Compound interest". You can use the means of compound interest to increase the return on your savings and investments, but it might also land you in trouble when you have interest compounding on the money you've lent. This basically means Compound interest can be used to your advantage or disadvantage.

The Meaning of Compound Interest

Compounding is indeed an essential means of growing. If you're acquainted with the "snowball effect," then you should understand how a thing can develop itself.

How Does the Concept Work?

One fundamental definition of Compound interest is "interest" gotten on a particular amount of money that was hitherto earned as "interest". This cycle leads to cumulative interest and account balances at an accumulative rate, otherwise referred to as *exponential growth*.

Let's begin with the idea of simple interest: you deposit money, and your bank account credits you with an interest on your initial deposit. For instance, you might deposit $100 for a year at 5 percent, and you get an interest of $5 over the year.

What happens the following year? This is where we bring in the theory of compounding You'll begin to get an interest on your original deposit, *and* you'll receive interest on the interest you just made.

It simply means that you'll earn *more* than $5 the following year because you now have a balance of $105, without having to make an initial deposit, so your earnings will speed up. At numerous banks, particularly online banks, there is compounding on your interests every day and it gets added to your account every month. This makes the movement of the entire process really fast.

You need to understand that borrowing money makes compounding work against you. The interest you have to pay on borrowed money increases your loan balance as time goes on, without having to borrow additional money.

How can you benefit from Compound Interest?

❖ **Save Timely and Regularly:** When multiplying your savings, you need to become friends with time. It takes some time to get enough drive, but that drive *will* definitely accrue and ultimately gain power. In some circumstances, beginning early means there is no need to save as much as somebody who *waits* to commence saving. Even if you abandon saving at some point, your head start can recompense dividends some other time. One thing you need to practice is how to be patient in order to let your money accrue and earn you an enormous amount in the future.

❖ **Check the APY.** Comparing bank products like savings accounts and CDs, you need to examine the annual percentage yield (APY). This considers compounding and also provides a factual yearly rate. Auspiciously, it's easy to discover because banks characteristically broadcast the APY since it's greater than the rate of interest. Endeavor to realize more money on your savings, however, it's almost certainly not worth substituting banks for an additional 0.10 percent except you have an enormously great account balance.

❖ **Rid yourself of Debts as early as possible and Pay More as soon as possible:** Disbursing as little on your dues, as you can may not really help you as a result of the fact that you might hardly make money in the interest charges and there could be an increase in your equilibrium. One mistake you would make as a student who has dues is to stay away from benefitting from interest charges and pay back your interest while it increases in order to avoid getting the shock of your life after valediction. Paying without being obligated to pay will definitely help you reduce your entire interest cost.

❖ **Continue to lend minimum rates:** While the interest rate on your dues can actually have an effect on your monthly dues, the growth of your debt can also be regulated and the period it requires to repay it all. It's challenging to put up with multiplied rates. Examine how sensible it is to amalgamate arrears and ensure your interest rate is lessened as your debt is paid.

You can increase your wealth through the method of Compounding. However, you need to know it isn't magical. In order to benefit from compounding, you need to commence with a particular amount of money, pledge it into an account, and watch your money accrue. To end up with any noteworthy savings, you should do this regularly, monthly and annually. The heavy lifting isn't accomplished by Compounding.

What makes compound interest dominant?

Repetition of payment actually enables Compounding. Starting out might not really impress you. However, there is an instant change as soon as your interest begins to accrue.

- ❖ **How Repeatedly:** The regularity of compounding is really essential. More recurrent compounding phases, every day, for instance, tend to have more significant outcomes. After deciding to own a savings account, you should especially choose accounts that accrue every day. You might merely comprehend interest expenses included in your account monthly. However, computations can be made every day. Some accounts only calculate interest once-a-month or annually.

- ❖ **How Time-consuming:** You can achieve more intensive compounding over extended time. Additionally, you realize an increased amount of payments to the account when you leave your earnings to accrue.

❖ **Supplementary Influences:** The interest rate is also an important influence in your account balance over time. Higher rates mean an account will mature more rapidly. However, sometimes a lot of people experience the situation where compound interest actually overcomes an amplified rate. Particularly, over extended phases, a compounded account and a reduced trifling rate might eventually have an increased equilibrium compared to the use of simple interest. Compute your analysis to determine what's going to happen and discover the breakeven point.

Your account balance can also be affected by certain extractions and payments, nonetheless, it is entirely different from compounding. Leaving your cash to accrue or frequently tallying fresh credits to your account performs well. When your profit is withdrawn, you diminish the outcome of compounding.

❖ Compounding isn't affected by how much money is involved. Whether you commence with a sum of $100 or one million dollars, it actually has an equivalent performance and your equilibrium is exactly the same when you plan the evolution carefully. The incomes appear larger when you begin with a huge payment. However, there is no penalty for beginning little or possessing accounts distinctly. It's pre-eminent to emphasize on *proportions and period* when preparing for future purpose. The amount you make becomes an outcome of your frequency and timeframe.

❖ **Regular compounding,** every day or periodic, actually assists you, however, do not be swayed by the frequency. When there is compounding on your interest every day, you continue to receive more or a reduced amount of the equal APY. For example, an account paying 5 percent APY doesn't pay 5 percent per day. You get 1/365th of 5 percent every day. Still, frequent compounding gives you a little edge to help your money mature more rapidly.

How to Calculate Compound Interest?

Compound interest can be calculated in various means to gain vision into how you can grasp your goals and help you keep accurate outlooks. When calculating, you need to imagine certain scenarios with different figures, and see the outcome if you save a little more or how much interest you would make as time goes on. There are several calculators online as well as financial calculators you could use yourself.

Make use of this formula to find compound interest.

A = P (1 + [r / n]) ^ not

To use this calculation, insert in the following variables:

* ❖ **A: this stands for your amount**

* ❖ **p:** your original deposit, referred to as the *principal*

* ❖ **r:** the yearly *interest rate.*

❖ **n:** this stands for the *number of compounding periods* yearly

❖ **t:** the amount of *time* that your money accumulates

Chapter 8

ADVANCED INVESTING STRATEGIES

Dogs of the Dow

Dogs of the Dow can be defined as an investment strategy which makes use of the 10-highest dividend–yielding stocks in the Dow Jones Industrial Average (DJIA) annually. Because the Dow is one of the ancient and most extensively charted directories globally — and commonly is seen as a measurement for the comprehensive market — it is not rare for market policymakers to base investing procedures on some apparatuses of the DJIA. The main motive to go with the Dogs is that it offers a direct procedure intended to execute unevenly in line with the Dow.

Dogs of the Dow Procedure

Dogs of the Dow is rooted in the fact that top-class firms do not change their dividend to replicate trading circumstances and, consequently, the dividend is a quota of the ordinary value of the company. In disparity, the stock price does waver during the course of the business progression. This should imply that firms with a great dividend comparative to stock price are near the end of their business phase, so their stock price is expected to upsurge quicker than firms with stumpy dividend yields. In this situation, an investor plowing his money in high-dividend-yielding firms per annum should outdo the general market.

Dividend stocks propose existing income and growth possibility, so no wonder many investors are fascinated with them. All the companies who are members of DJIA are dividend-paying companies who are also among the most important blue-chip businesses in the universal economy. There are several means of obtaining these securities. You can select individual stocks and construct your own collection; invest openly in the Dow via ETFS or instead of putting your money in the whole Dow. You can go with the Dogs of the Dow approach, whose stocks propose healthier yields than the Dow itself. Over and over again, the Dogs have managed to overtake the Dow over the progression of the year.

How Does Dogs of the Dow Approach Work?

The general idea is to make the stock selection an easy process safe process, the concluding one because the world is limited to first-class stocks. As a policy, Dogs of the Dow works this way: After the stock market finishes on the last day of the year, hand-pick the 10-best dividend-yielding stocks in the DJIA. Then, on the initial trading day of the fresh year, invest an equivalent dollar sum in each of them. Keep the portfolio for close to a year, then reapply the procedure at the commencement of each succeeding year.

For most amateurs, though, investing is never as easy as that, specifically with the innumerable approaches out there. So, it befits the regular individual investor to recognize what they are doing with their money. Hence, Dogs of the Dow tools flourish. Just look through the web to see Dogs of the Dow ideas, clarification, scrutinizes, calculators, strategies, forecasts, you could also browse through a Dogs of the Dow website.

Dividend capture strategy

The dividend capture strategy can be defined as an income-focused stock trading strategy prevalent among day dealers. Unlike other traditional methods, which are concerned with purchasing and keeping constant dividend-paying shares to creäte a fixed income stream, it is an energetic trading plan that necessitates recurrent purchasing and trading of shares, keeping them for only a while—just long enough to seize the dividend paid by the stock. The principal stock could occasionally be held for just a particular day.

Companies pay out dividends per annum or four times a year, but some are remunerated monthly. Traders who make use of dividend capture strategy have a preference for the larger yearly dividend disbursements, as it is usually stress-free to make the strategy lucrative with loftier dividend amounts. Dividend calendars with data on dividend payouts are freely accessible on any number of monetary websites.

Dividend timeframe

There are four important dates connected with dividend capture strategy.

- ❖ **Declaration date:** This is the date when the firm announces its dividend. It happens well at the payment upfront.

- ❖ **Ex-dividend date (or ex-date):** This is the deadline for being qualified to get the dividend payment. There is also a drop in the stock price on this day, in consensus with the declared dividend sum. Traders are advised to obtain the stock preceding this critical day.

- ❖ **Date of record:** This is the day when the qualified shareholders to be paid dividends are recorded by the firm.

- ❖ **Pay date:** This is the day when the dividend payment is made.

- ❖ **Declaration Date:** This is the day dividend payment is announced by the Board of directors.

- ❖ **Ex-Date (or Ex-Dividend Date):** The security begins trading without the dividend.

- ❖ **Date of Record:** This is the day dividend is received by Current stockholders on record.

- ❖ **Pay Date:** This is the day the payment of the dividend is issued.

How the Strategy Works

One very appealing thing about the dividend capture strategy is its straightforwardness—no difficult fundamental analysis or charting is mandatory. Fundamentally, an investor or trader procures shares of the stock before the ex-dividend date and trades the shares on the ex-dividend date or any time afterward. If the share price does plummet after the dividend declaration, the investor may wait until the price springs back to its initial worth. Investors do not have to keep the stock until the pay date comes for the payment of dividend

Hypothetically, the dividend capture strategy doesn't seem to make much sense. If the market is activated with impeccable logic, then the dividend amount would be exactly replicated in the share price pending the ex-dividend date, when the stock price would plummet by accurately the dividend sum. Meanwhile, markets do not function with such accurate precision, it doesn't typically work like that. Most often, a trader gets a considerable portion of the dividend in spite of trading the stock at a slight forfeiture succeeding the ex-dividend date. A distinctive example would be a stock trading at $20 per share, paying a $1 dividend, dropping in price on the ex-date only downcast to $19.50, which allows a trader to realize some net earnings of $0.50, positively capturing half the dividend in return.

Chapter 9

DIVIDEND INVESTING TIPS

Putting your money in dividend-paying stock is a calculated means of establishing a dependable income stream and building a passive income. Although investing can be a very risky thing, there is a great possibility of earning massive returns from investing.

It is not difficult to become a successful investor, however, it actually requires a comprehensive knowledge of certain ideologies. Below are some of the things you should consider while investing.

Select Quality instead of Quantity

One of the most imperative deliberations for depositors when selecting investments is the dividend yield. The sophisticated the yield, the healthier the profit, but the statistics can be elusive. If the stock's contemporary payout level is not justifiable over the durable, those market-beating dividends can rapidly dry up. REITs are good instances of how instabilities in the market can openly have emotional impact on dividend payouts.

Choosing an investment that boasts of great stability may imply forfeiting a convinced quantity of yield in the temporary, but the result may be more encouraging, predominantly for investors who have a preference for a buy-and-hold tactic. The income produced by lower-risk dividend stocks may be lesser, but it's possible to be more dependable over time.

❖ Stick with Established Companies: The stock market interchanges in series and it has an inclination of repeating itself every time. When selecting dividend investments, there's no healthier evaluating stick than a stock's previous presentation. Explicitly, stockholders should be directing those companies that have attained a "dividend aristocrat" position.

These are renowned companies that have amplified their dividend disbursements to shareholders unswervingly over the preceding 25 years. Their varieties are easily distinguishable, and they produce a stable flow of cash with an extraordinary possibility of permanently doing so in the future.

Observe the development prospect

While innovative corporations can pay out some remarkable dividends, stockholders shouldn't be making decisions without first conducting thorough research. Apart from observing the previous and current returns, it's also very essential to observe the corporation's impending prospective to intensify its dividend payouts.

This is the principal dissimilarity between growth investing and worth investing. With growth investing, instead of concentrating on what the stock is dealing in presently, you would observe the abiding viewpoint for development to measure how lucrative it would be from a dividend perspective.

Pay attention to the Payout Ratio

The safety of the company's investment is sometimes revealed by its payment ratio. This reveals the amount paid out to investors as well as the amount of income retained by the firm.

If you ever come across a high-yield dividend stock, but the corporation is paying out a significant proportion of its revenue to depositors, that's a red flag that you should be really careful. If the firm were to see its revenue stream abridged, the aggregate of dividends you're getting would go on the chopping block.

Diversify

There's an intensive argument to be made for directing assets on a bit of stocks or leveling a detailed segment of the market. If the businesses or corporation you've zeroed in on have an outstanding track record, that promises well for your forthcoming dividend earnings. Meanwhile, that can be challenging in the course of a market downtown.

One way to diversify your income is to spread assets over several dividend-paying investments, allowing you to reduce risk. When dividends are abridged in a particular area, you might not really feel the loss because your other portfolio keeps performing.

Understand when you need to give up

Investing expert Warren Buffett confidently believes in looking into the future when it comes to investing, but like any keen investor, he knows when to cut his losses. You have to understand the difference between having to wait for an investment to pay off and being there for too long. This can be an easy mistake to make when buying stocks that on the surface appear to be a great value. The problem usually occurs when the company itself tends to fail to deliver regarding growth. You should be able to tell when a stock is going down the drain, but you also need to know when to act on it and when to buckle up.

Conclusion

Well, I hope you enjoyed this book and got plenty of value from it to go and kick start your dividend investing portfolio. But remember, with the tactics and methods taught in this book, you can enhance your portfolio with an exponential amount of value. All you need to do is to work on your evaluation and analytical skills in order to decipher companies who offer the best returns while abating risk and diversifying your income.

It's nothing short of a manipulating act, but by obeying the afore-mentioned guidelines, investors may train themselves to become really successful and financially stable for the future.

www.ingramcontent.com/pod-product-compliance
Lightning Source LLC
Chambersburg PA
CBHW030509210326
41597CB00013B/848